**Dos X**

**LATINX: THE FUTURE IS NOW**

A series edited by Lorgia García-Peña and Nicole Guidotti-Hernández

**BOOKS IN THE SERIES**

PJ DiPietro, *Sideways Selves: Travesti and Jotería Struggles across the Américas*

Sharina Maíllo-Pozo, *Bridging Sonic Borders: Popular Music in Contemporary Dominican/Dominicanyork Literature*

Frank García, *Clicas: Gender, Sexuality and Struggle in Latina/o/x Gang Literature and Film*

Regina Marie Mills, *Invisibility and Influence: A Literary History of AfroLatinidades*

Jason Ruiz, *Narcomedia: Latinidad, Popular Culture, and America's War on Drugs*

Rebeca L. Hey-Colón, *Channeling Knowledges: Water and Afro-Diasporic Spirits in Latinx and Caribbean Worlds*

Tatiana Reinoza, *Reclaiming the Americas: Latinx Art and the Politics of Territory*

Kristy L. Ulibarri, *Visible Borders, Invisible Economies: Living Death in Latinx Narratives*

Marisel C. Moreno, *Crossing Waters: Undocumented Migration in Hispanophone Caribbean and Latinx Literature and Art*

Yajaira M. Padilla, *From Threatening Guerrillas to Forever Illegals: US Central Americans and the Cultural Politics of Non-Belonging*

Francisco J. Galarte, *Brown Trans Figurations: Rethinking Race, Gender, and Sexuality in Chicanx/Latinx Studies*

# Dos X

## *Disability and Racial Dysphoria in Latinx and Filipinx Culture*

Sony Coráñez Bolton

University of Texas Press
*Austin*

Printed in the United States of America
First edition, 2025



∞ The paper used in this book meets the minimum requirements of ANSI/NISO Z39.48-1992 (R1997) (Permanence of Paper).

Library of Congress Cataloging-in-Publication Data

Names: Coráñez Bolton, Sony, 1985– author.
Title: Dos X : disability and racial dysphoria in Latinx and Filipinx culture / Sony Coráñez Bolton.
Other titles: Latinx (Series)
Description: First edition. | Austin : University of Texas Press, 2025. | Series: Latinx: the future is now | Includes bibliographical references and index.
Identifiers: LCCN 2024031460 (print) | LCCN 2024031461 (ebook)
ISBN 978-1-4773-3136-1 (hardcover)
ISBN 978-1-4773-3137-8 (paperback)
ISBN 978-1-4773-3138-5 (pdf)
ISBN 978-1-4773-3139-2 (epub)
Subjects: LCSH: Vargas, Jose Antonio—Criticism and interpretation. | Bulosan, Carlos—Criticism and interpretation. | Roley, Brian Ascalon—Criticism and interpretation. | Filipino Americans—Ethnic identity—Case studies. | Filipinos—United States—Ethnic identity—Case studies. | Passing (Identity)—United States—Case studies. | Latin Americans—United States—Ethnic identity—Case studies. | Disabilities—Philosophy. | Capitalism—Philosophy. | Language and languages—Political aspects. | Frontier thesis. | Spain—Colonies—Ethnic relations. | LCGFT: Case studies.
Classification: LCC E184.F4 C665 2025 (print) | LCC E184.F4 (ebook) | DDC 305.899/21073—dc23/eng/20241218
LC record available at https://lccn.loc.gov/2024031460
LC ebook record available at https://lccn.loc.gov/2024031461

*To all the mongrels.*

# Contents

# Illustrations

# Preface
## *The great bracero*

two pairs of brown eyes lock & bloom light across a shared iris
both helix photons in chainlinks up the backs of their retinas

one once a boy from yucatán who drank up sunrises on the gulf of méxico
as a child he slurps up paletas and coughs sweetly from too much cinnamon in the rice milk

he would spend summers near the altepetl from which la malinche was ripped away
he would frequent the banks of the coatzacoalcos once navigated by jade serpent gods

across the border the boy would then pick grapes with calloused hands threading vines
his nostrils caked with desert sands wafting down from the stratosphere like snow

their iris a mirror etched from pale diaphanous glass, a portal with another
hand anchored on its burnished surface. the hand, same hue, pushes

away. a way forward as a bracero of a different variety, with a different path
the other arm of the alien body that crossed the pacific. his ilocano hands grasp

and tug roots. he cradled the volcanic soils of pineapple plantations.
in the before,
his life was on islands mischievously skipping on the cobblestones of
vigan. life was

lazy afternoons in the arms of his father swinging in hemp-hewn
hammocks. he would pray
novenas on his knees for fiesta days to san isidro, patron saint of labor.

& now the boys of the iris live at both ends of the same grapevine
lassoing a big world.
their lives entwine in fields of central california. filipino mexico
fluoresces like an aurora

across once opaque oceans made clear. rough hands clasp both arms
of the greater bracero.
they meet in a tender embrace. sunburnt bodies kiss enfolding and
collapsing into each other.

# Dos X

# INTRODUCTION
## *Racial Dysphoria*

When I was sixteen years old, I worked in a health and wellness club for the wealthy in Lake Forest, Illinois. This was my first real job as a high schooler. I made approximately twelve dollars an hour washing and folding towels. My father worked as a mechanic there and put me up for the job. I maintained the men's locker room by wiping down surfaces, cleaning toilets—sometimes flushing them on behalf of those that could not be bothered—replacing shampoo and conditioner, and picking up clients' used towels. I worked about twenty hours a week on the weekends, and would study in between breaks. My father and I were actually coworkers, which is a strange observation to make now in my thirties. We were bonded together in an atypical blue-collar working arrangement in the midst of immense wealth. Such camaraderie might imply some kind of sameness between my father and me. However, my father is a white man with a brown son. This contrast was the setting of an emerging double racial consciousness for me. Such an emergence was circumscribed by a muddled shared reality of intersecting brownness.

The locker-room attending staff were all Mexican immigrants except for me. As a student of Spanish, I was eager to communicate, to understand, and to be understood. It made work smoother and even fun. Daily, by the rich clientele, I was greeted with "hola," thanked with "gracias," and asked questions about where in Mexico I was from and when I came to the United States. Sometimes I received requests to attend to something in the locker room in broken Spanish. The assumption may have been that I did not speak English fluently, as was indeed the case with the staff of recent immigrants with whom I worked. My perceptions of others' perceptions of me were also often mediated by my father's observations of my coworkers: "I have never met a harder working group of people in my life." Thus my growing associations with "Mexicanness" (associations with which I was also becoming associated) were largely positive. The language of "microaggressions" was not well circulated, nor as mainstream as it is today. Even the questions I did receive as a brown face in a rather white space were ones that I did and could answer; I did immigrate to the United States at a young age with my mother, but from a different Spanish colony.

Years later, I would read Octavio Paz's philosophical ruminations about Mexican (masculine) identity as an impenetrable labyrinth of introspective solitude.[1] These potentially homophobic observations would strike me askance as a queer Filipino person; I felt open not only to the penetrative politics of the world via my queerness but also to the multivalent constructedness of my brownness. I say the following with ample interpretive license and only as a way to forge productive solidarities through the iterative and multiple itineraries of brown racialization: I feel convinced that my experience as a Filipino, in the linguistic, postcolonial, and US multiracial theater I have been recounting, can be described as being a "queer Mexican"—that is, someone who (through stereotypical associative meanings many might have about labor, appearance, and the use of language) one would be surprised is not Latino. What might it mean to categorize a Filipino as a "queer Mexican"? I was someone brought into a racial recognition as a "Mexican" who is not and does not identify as such. But this describes, to my mind, a particular and multifarious kind of conscripted racial drag that activates the historical situatedness of shared colonial encounters and intersecting migration politics. Nevertheless, this history goes back much further. The Philippines was, administratively speaking, a part of Mexico as it was managed through the Viceroyalty of New Spain from 1565 to 1815. In the broadest and most global colonial sense, some itineraries of Philippine history could be considered extensions of Mexican history, as these places were chained together in a more or less contiguous political and economic imaginary. I do not mean to suggest that, in carrying the trace of these borrowings, Philippine languages like Tagalog are somehow dialects of Mexican Spanish—though I must admit I am excited by that framing. Rather, such linguistic connections demonstrate that Philippine and Mexican historical experiences are not completely discrete. It is, as Paula Park argues in the context of Philippine and Latin American literary and cultural exchanges, that while "national borders have been effectively contested, interrogated and reimagined, giving rise to hemispheric, transnational and even global approaches to literary production . . . geographical designations . . . have persisted." She observes that these "seemingly more rational, continental and subcontinental divisions of the world have led to rigid academic compartmentalization."[2] Park demonstrates that this state of affairs is why Latin Americanists have ignored, for instance, Spanish-language literature or Hispanic cultural production from the Philippines because of the teleological emphasis on reifying an imagined region of the world that we call Latin America. I want to advance this conversation from the purview of global Hispanophone literary studies to thinking about the braided experiences of migrant cultural archives within the United States. *Dos X* will demonstrate the contemporary itineraries of such overlaps with special attention to Mexican-Filipino connections, while also thinking through broader Latinx and Filipinx intersections.

In the contemporary milieu I am describing, these are brown bodies that are embedded in a racial political economy prioritizing the use of migrant physical capacities and dispensing with them in potentially extractive and hierarchical ways. The meanings of my body extended into migrant imaginaries that are constructed through and as Mexican American. The body is thus, I would suggest, part (even a small—and perhaps the smallest—part) of that archive. My laboring body was viewed as indistinguishable from the Mexicans I worked with, due to its material enmeshment with an immigrant landscape that was consistent with the dominant racial politics of the Chicagoland area at the time.

## On the "Misrecognitive": Embracing an Analytic of Racial Dysphoria

The argument of *Dos X* is that racial misrecognition constitutes its own sort of epistemology and aesthetic. And, thus, it can potentiate different kinds of ethical and political relations. I suggest that racial misrecognition is a unique variety of epistemic disclosure because 1. you question the knowledge that another has about the kind of body or person that you are, and 2. you may need to imagine a diverse apparatus of diagnostic criteria to understand the other entity with whom you are collapsed. Misrecognition is a unique kind of experience, in the sense of it indexing a heightened awareness of yourself as a particular subject of history *and* how you are an object of the multiplicities of *stories*—as disaggregated as they may be—via the gaze of another. The radical dislodging from one's identitarian location by the cognition of another necessarily and definitionally binds one's cognition to that of others—this might be the primary function of misre*cognition* that I wish to highlight throughout the book. At base, I maintain that misrecognition can potentiate other kinds of ethical relations with the world and the people in it, thus constructing an apprehension of similitude that bears the trace of the difference that you might desire. This difference disentangles you from and resists what we might label as the "misrecognitive" faculties of another.

This misrecognitive space is an important epistemological crossroads that produces what I identify throughout this project as an affect-aesthetic of *racial dysphoria*. This is an affect and aesthetic that I track throughout the various case studies of the book through visual, social, and linguistic inventories of literary and cultural production. Racial dysphoria describes moments of racial misrecognition wherein one becomes uncanny to oneself or many become uncanny to themselves. This racial uncanny registers an agency and intention toward the other that is paradoxically anchored to the epistemological uncertainty produced through misrecognition. But it can only do so if we bring different ethical parameters to our navigations of these misrecognitive moments, which, I suggest, can articulate a history of the present that understands the social, historical, and political forces that have shaped the conditions of possibility for that misrecognition in the first place. In the literary and cultural artifacts that I analyze in *Dos X*, misrecognition produces dysphoric attachments to identity that often disarticulate one from the provincialism of self, thus surfacing more critical understandings of one's relation to the modes of production in racial capitalism. This, I argue, is the main engine driving racial interchangeability. In other words, there is an uncanny sense that you have when being racially misrecognized as another, which surfaces an aesthetic and intuitive confrontation with your mutually shared position within the social, political, and economic organization of racial capitalism. For instance, I was misrecognized as "Mexican," thereby indexing a shared positionality as particular kinds of racialized bodies that have historically been used, extracted, and even placed in similar geographies, in order to further the mandates of racial capital. So, there is a lot that the misrecognitive gets absolutely right if we orient ourselves outside of the provincialism of "correct" identification.

Racial dysphoria can refer to the epistemological anxieties of misidentification. However, the dysphoria of race can also be a heuristic that lenses such uncanny moments through the filter of shared colonial, political, and historical encounter. Returning to the personal account with which I began: rather than reject the misapprehension of my being "Mexican" due either to the negative stereotypes associated with Latino immigrants or even to some kind of progressive stance against racist misrecognition ("you dare assume we all look alike?"), I became even more interested in learning Spanish and, later, embraced the social conditions that shaped mistaken identifications of this variety. I did so neither to complete nor somehow to materialize the racial drag I was conscripted into. Quite to the contrary, as later I would discover that learning Spanish became an important avenue for me to study my Asian American identity as an Asian subject from a former Spanish colony. To paraphrase Gayatri Spivak: I did my homework. I do not attest to this because I am somehow more strongly moral or uniquely ethical in some way. I state it to pose a question about the ways that we mark the lines of connection between groups. What might it mean to feel a true sense of solidarity with one another or to possess an avid interest in the destiny of another group to which you do not belong? What I call racial dysphoria potentiates different kinds of ethical encounters with others with whom you are rendered interchangeable. But you confront an ethical relation with them precisely because you are not them. Neither do you belong to the communities that they hail from but, despite this—or, especially, because of it—one ought to care about them anyway. Misrecognition allows for a diagnostic reckoning with the social, political, and economic conditions that collapse visual and political registers of racialization into a unitary amalgam.

I argue that the sense of racial dysphoria that follows racial misrecognition is an affective sense that allows us to diagnose the contours of racial capitalism and its various ableist tactics of racialization. Following the work of disability theorist Lennard J. Davis, it is clear that capitalism requires the statistical normalization of the body to facilitate the extraction of surplus value.[3] For surplus value to be generated, labor must be reduced to uniform and interchangeable units of labor time. Following Marx's arguments on the fabrication of value as an embedded sociological feature of objects turned into commodities, we see that this commodity fetishism requires the interchangeability of units of socially agreed upon labor-time. Otherwise, no stable sense of value would be produced through uniformly measured amounts of labor. This has implications for the bodies that dispense physical capacity that we capture as "work" or "labor." "Work" measures the utility of the body to capitalist systems of production. There cannot be wild statistical variations on the expectations of what a body—or particular kinds of bodies—may produce under certain controlled conditions. Biopolitical norms emerge to satisfy structural requirements for sameness in the name of efficiency. This is also about time. Bodies and their uniqueness must collapse into the numerical sameness that temporal logics of capital demand. Reading the realities of race into that equation, it seems that with the biopolitical optimization of the laborer to comply with the regnant conception of capitalist embodiment, it is indeed inevitable that brown bodies would be rendered interchangeable with one another. Such interchangeability is a structural feature of both racial ableist capitalism and its management of "alien" bodies, rather than being epiphenomenal to them. I suggest that the racial dysphoria produced in moments of misrecognition is a sensing of the structure of interchangeability that adumbrates racial ableist capitalism.

Why is this about ableism? *Dos X* reorients a fundamental argument in ethnic studies scholarship over the past three decades. The work of scholars like Iyko Day, Denise Ferreira da Silva, Beth Lew-Williams, Lisa Lowe, Mae M. Ngai, Nayan Shah, and Ronald T. Takaki has articulated well that the fiction of the universalism of citizenship structurally depends on a racial underclass of alien labor.[4] As an inclusive liberal franchise of rights to property and self-actualization, citizenship requires the structural exclusion of aliens whose labors maintain the fictions of inclusive liberal humanism. As Lowe has foundationally argued, the franchise of citizenship has relied historically on the paradoxical exclusion of immigrants from its supposedly universalist auspices. Such exclusion is fundamentally about ability. The freedom, autonomy, and sovereignty of the US citizen require an extractive relation with the physical capacities of racialized migrant labor to subsidize the able-bodied independence of citizenship. Working off of the arguments presented by literary scholar Julie Avril Minich, the alien-raced body is the substrate and racial infrastructure upon which the fictively independent citizen rests.[5] We see this physical ableist divide play out in many industries of creative labor. The innovative potential of capitalism, the office job, and the maintenance of a global middle consumerist class that has reached the highest heights of educational attainment are all manifestations of an extractive relationship to an alien body who performs physical labors that we need not. The unitary and interchangeable nature of their labor time, which is a function of the racialization of such bodies as capital, facilitates the ostensibly autonomous ingenuity of an ever-ascending class of wealthier consumers. Racial misrecognition is a puncture in this system of structurally engineered atomistic interchangeability that I hope to interrupt, thus linking the philosophical complexity of misrecognition to some central debates in immigration and disability histories.

The link between foreignness, citizenship, and disability has been long established in immigration studies. Scholars such as Douglas Baynton, Margot Canaday, Paul K. Longmore, Kim E. Nielsen, Nayan Shah, and Lauri Umansky have work that collectively demonstrates the ways that perversity, contagion, and dysfunction have shaped immigration politics and history.[6] Sexual perversion and physical deformities were often used by state officials to determine which immigrants were "good" and which were "bad." "Good" referred to productive potential citizens whose labors could contribute advantage to the citizens of the United States. "Bad," as established by the historical work of Baynton and Canaday, often suggested the potential danger of "malformed" individuals becoming wards of the state. Ableism, which is defined as the structural and personal preference for able-bodiedness, is then a vital ideology in shaping the historical pathways for immigration and thus who the state fabricates as ideal citizens, what their bodies should look like, and what labors they ought to dispense on behalf of society. Shah has notably demonstrated the ways that contagion, disease, and illness were fundamental discourses integral to Chinese and South Asian racialization on the west coast.[7] Disability and the disabling effects of American capitalism were systematically imposed to exclude swaths of the population from the vaunted position of the citizen, while the citizen (as a structure and ideology) depended on that excluded labor to mortgage their individual existence as "free." And while not about immigration per se, scholars like Jessica Cowing and Susan Burch have crucially demonstrated how settler colonialism animated a settler desire for land and Indigenous resources through the production and tactical use of disability.[8] Because the state formation that makes determinations on the quality of the migrants coming to US shores is itself a settler colonial construction, these are important perspectives to consider. Cowing calls this dynamic "settler ableism."[9] If the settler state is a fundamentally ableist institution that has justified dispossession of land through mythic constructions of Indian inability to be proper stewards of their own lands, then to see similar strategies used in immigration histories to adjudicate "good," healthy immigrants from "bad," defective ones is unsurprising. I cover some of this ground on the settler origins of US racial ableism in this project's first chapter. The ways that ableism structured US desire for Mexican territories is the epistemological ground upon which transpacific conquest was positioned, thus implicating the Philippines. It is historical crossroads such as these that condition the kinds of misrecognition nourished by a colonial racial ableism.

I make my argument by centering peculiar—though not

exceptional—forms of misrecognition that materialize between Filipinx and Latinx peoples in US multiethnic literature and culture. While I used "Filipino" to describe my own experiences above, I maintain the use of "x" in these identity formations not only to highlight the queerness of recognition, but also to signpost the racial instability that inheres within supposedly monolithic and seemingly coherent ethnonational constructions of self. The variability connoted by the mathematical metaphor of x is meant to highlight such mutabilities in the sphere of identification. Thus, it fits well as one of many rubrics to understand Filipinx representation—a central archive serving as the spine of this study. The motifs of identity shifting, chameleonic passing, and what I would consider moments of racial error are not uncommon in Filipinx American cultural and literary production. While I neither consider nor intend *Dos X* to be an exhaustive archive, we can see the development of this theme in the works of Filipino Americans Jose Antonio Vargas, Carlos Bulosan, and Brian Ascalon Roley—authors I cover in the case studies of this book.

Racial ambivalence is not a new topic in Filipinx American studies. Elsewhere, for instance, I have written (as have scholars like Sarita See and Victor Román Mendoza) about ambivalent racial formation in *Dogeaters*, the foundational postmodern Filipino novel by Jessica Hagedorn—attending to the iconic mestizo characters of Rio Gonzaga and, *especially*, of the Afro-Filipino Joey Sands.[10] My analysis of this peripatetic racialization is also reflected in the scholarly work of Alicia Arrizón, Rudy P. Guevarra Jr., Allan Punzalan Isaac, Long Le-Khac, and Anthony Christian Ocampo.[11] According to literary critic Martin Joseph Ponce, such multivalence is part of the reason for the proliferation of a Filipinx literary aesthetic that is routed through multiple forms of address, rather than unitary or unidirectional ones.[12] It is this plurivocality that I wish to explore much more explicitly within the context of misrecognition of one racial group for another; I wish to mine this tendency for its philosophical implications in the arena of giving a seemingly empirical account of oneself. Race seems to connote more "durable" criteria of identification than, say, the queer questioning that the performative category of gender has undergone in the past three decades.[13] This reality might be best illustrated by the fact that transgender identities have obtained more as valid expressions of mutable selfhood than have transracial identities in the sense of one race permanently identifying as another. Permanence here connotes that there can be a shared reality sustained as a temporal durational fact about a person who is transracial.[14] Instead, we see cases of race grifters like Rachel Dolezal, Jessica Krug, and the robust list of

"Pretendians" in indigenous societies within the borders of the US and Canada. Without endorsing or advocating for transracial identification per se, I am curious about similar phenomenological experiences of racial shifting that might speak to and help us navigate this impasse between the righteous and empirical reality of transgender identity on one hand and the appropriative lie of transracial identity on the other. At the same time, though, I wish to explain a fundamental difference between the racial shifting that I examine in this book and that of the cases of misrepresentation exemplified by the likes of Dolezal and Krug.

Adding my voice to the chorus of specifically Filipinx American racial ambiguity, I engaged with one possible origin for such ambivalence in my first book.[15] I took up the history and cultural discourse of Philippine *mestizaje* wherein multiple and sometimes contradictory racial formations coalesced in the production of a Filipino national identity as a racial account of political selfhood. The countervailing effects of both Spanish history and US colonial history are many times surfaced in these moments of misrecognition that I home in upon. Therefore, a main argument of this book is that racial error gets something "right" in the moment of misrecognition. In order to embrace the good epistemological grounds that racial error allows us to stand on, I would like to give some space to think about the reasonable yet misguided alternative: I suggest a productive suspension of what I call "identity empiricism."

## Identity Empiricism

For the time being and for the purposes of this study, I suspend the desire for what I call "identity empiricism." I define identity empiricism as the non-arbitrary but ultimately short-sighted reflex to always correct misapprehension by another such that your self-claimed identity meshes seamlessly with what you ideate as the shared reality of your existence. I suggest that self-disclosure functions at times more like a self-enclosure, thus placing barriers whose purpose is to navigate the anxiety of potential misclassification. Again, this is not an arbitrary predilection. We want to be seen for who we really are. Nevertheless, breaking down the ideologies, logics, and stakes of a question like "Who are you really?" or "Who am I really?" furnishes a philosophical complexity that is far from straightforward. One implication for such retreats into an "empirical" self, I argue, is to abandon the contextual parameters that shape the etiologies of self. I do not, however, argue for some sort of identity relativism. Some might be rightfully skeptical that many misrecognitions are often politically and socially engineered—such as those of so-called "Pretendians" or other race grifters that masquerade as another identity, availing themselves of resources that are allocated for marginalized groups. For these instances, "correction" and precision are vital. In this book, when I am referring to racial drag and performativity, I am not speaking about these kinds of socially manufactured misrecognitions that often do not bear the trace of connected colonial genealogies of mixture. Instead, when historicized, they are only found to be more or less a singular misrecognitive chain. That is to say, the act of misrecognition was *the* volitional purpose that involved an active performative dispensation of race as an individualized technology of self. For instance, this can be seen in cases of "playing Indian" and analogous racial masquerade such as blackface and minstrelsy.[16] Also apropos is the genealogy of yellowfacing in cinematic history. While endlessly fascinating and certainly relevant to the framework of *Dos X*, this is not the sort of transraciality that I emphasize.

I do believe that much more work and thinking needs to be done excavating the ethical parameters and potentially meaningful ways that transracial identities *could* manifest (that mirror transgender ones without collapsing important distinctions). Here, however, I am interested specifically in modes of racial drag bearing the trace of colonial processes that are global in scope, thus melding geographies and braiding migratory histories. In the context of Filipinx-Latinx cultural politics, I ask: What can be gleaned from "leaning into" such moments of misrecognition, rather than reflexively correcting them? In posing this question, I also wish to highlight its fundamental similarity to, rather than difference from, Indigenous critiques of Pretendianism. That is, as Kim TallBear has suggested, Indigenous identification often vexes western empiricism because it is collectivist in ethos, rather than individualist.[17]

The kinds of social and ethical relations I suggest that racial misrecognition can constellate are precisely non-individualist in nature. Identity-grift is made possible by an individualist conception of selfhood—as in: I claim I am x and it is morally wrong of you to submit such a claim to scrutiny, as it disrespects my personal experiences. Experience and identity claims become opaque, and not only are they rendered impervious to ethical dissection, but this rendering is in itself labeled unethical. On the other hand, in collectivist conceptions of identity, it is all too common and even right to ask: Who are you? Where do you hail from? Who are your parents and grandparents? In and with whom do you anchor your claims of identity? Your personal feelings and experiences of self, while important, are not sufficient conditions to claim an identity, particularly if such a claim would contravene the material citizenship or sovereignty of another community. For instance, it would be ludicrous for me to claim that I am Estonian or Italian without materially grounding those claims in a shared and meaningful conception of those identity markers. Such an argument parallels the various false claims to Cherokee, Mohawk, or Chickasaw identities (and others) that all too often strangle sovereign national practices to determine citizenship. As a citizen of a former Spanish colony, however, I could claim Spanish national identity through certain bureaucratic processes that are redressive in nature—it is more along *these* lines that I would anchor the framework of this book.

And while this book is not about Indigenous sovereignty and identity practices in the main, I think collectivist responses and demands for accountability are helpful for thinking outside of the individualistic enclosures we place around identity. One might read Indigenous callouts of fraudulent Pretendians as exclusionary. I actually read such sovereign practices of bringing individuals to account as foundationally grounded in solidarity, relationality, and being in an intentional community. They are, in actuality, invitational. A concrete example is Adrienne Keene's letter to Elizabeth Hoover, the UC Berkeley professor that claimed Mohawk and Mi'kmaq descent.[18] In it, Keene makes abundantly clear that she did research into Hoover's claims not to ruin her:

> [Hoover] has continued, publicly and in small groups, to reference "somebody" or "a colleague" who did the research into her family, and in some cases implied that it was research done out of spite or vindictive in nature. That "somebody" was me, and this research came from the exact opposite of spite or hate—I just wanted to know the truth, and I truly thought the answer would be different than what I found.[19]

Keene also noted that she "offered to help [Hoover] write a statement about her identity to clear things up," which the latter ultimately declined. And, indeed, as a non-native person observing and engaging with these accountability processes, what is really most helpful to understand is that, often, the native people that do the labor to clarify family genealogy demonstrate a care for the masquerader's ancestors in ways that the subject of inquiry does not:

> I also feel strangely and illogically protective over these random white ancestors [of Hoover's], who I now feel connected to over months of

> reading their lives through online documents and tracing the trails and trials they endured. There is tragedy and sadness here. Though they are not Indigenous and they are not my family relations, they didn't ask to be pulled into this. However, in making these claims about herself in print and in public, in accepting opportunities designated for Indigenous peoples, Liz [Hoover] pulled them into this.[20]

What would it mean to simply care about Indigenous issues, familiarize oneself with histories of settler colonialism, and understand the various relations between First Nations or First Peoples and the state, rather than be overwhelmed with the desire to stake an empirical claim to such identity? Why is that a necessary condition to do the work of relationality? This is why the actions of racial pretenders like Hoover, Rachel Dolezal, and Jessica Krug are so harmful: because any positive work or even deeply and genuinely felt affinity they had with the Mohawk, Black American, and Latinx communities, respectively, become bound up and inoculated by the lie of impersonation.

Perhaps one could genuinely internalize and articulate a "transracial" identity. Speaking personally, I might consider the claims to Filipino identity of someone for whom a shared understanding of their Filipino-ness is not, at first blush, materially grounded. What I wish to point out in these instances of racial masquerade—and what has been deemed as racial theft of resources—is one overriding problem in all of these cases: the overwhelming, pervasive, and, ultimately, pernicious western need to lay individualist and ironically opaque empiricist claims to identity in the first place. I do not want to be misunderstood here. In actuality, I do not find the claims of or to a racial identity that is other than the one with which you have been born or ascribed from birth particularly or uniquely problematic, per se. This might be surprising and shocking to read, but I do not want to say it is absolutely impossible for people to meaningfully hold to such an identity claim, and that, culturally, we might witness a proliferation of "transracial" individuals. However, such claims would neither supersede in importance nor serve as a substitute for materially grounded solidarity, redistributive practices, and the meaningful reallocation of resources whose initial distribution follows settler and racial hierarchies. A mere claiming of another identity does not change the reality of this material background.

While the preceding paragraph might indicate otherwise, *Dos X* is not squarely about transraciality. Nevertheless, in ideating and presenting on the project, this question has come up continuously. While I examine some instances where the volitional act of taking up an identity through speech and dress does come up, my main concern is more around instances of unintentional conscription into racial drag. This, I suggest, is a structural feature of racial ableist capitalism and thus exceeds individuated and personal will. By reflecting on misrecognitive politics in this way, we can answer a rather straightforward question: What is it about the structure of racial capitalism that leads to misrecognition and interchange of one body for another in the first place? How might the cultural-literary economy of texts that is meant to represent these interactions be fertile ground to mount other modes of relationality using misrecognition as a starting point? For this project, as I will explore, the answer to these questions partly lies in the mutually reinforcing structures of ableism and racial capitalism. For now, however, I wish to outline my own personal stakes in and genesis of this project, which go beyond early moments of racial drag in my life: I am often misrecognized as Latino.

## Dos X: Toward a Philosophy of Being

As a Filipino American, my line of work and scholarship has involved the use of Spanish and the exploration of Hispanic American archives as they have shaped Philippine experiences of race. This has historically produced slippages of identification in which the shared realities in which the terms Filipino, Philippine, and Filipinx attempt to articulate durable empirical filiation, and meld with (or become commensurate with) Latinx or Latin American racial formations. As I will demonstrate through the cultural archive of this book, my ethnographic experience as an ambiguous and ostensible Latino is not epiphenomenal or idiosyncratic. Rather, it is part of an enduring and important structure of sentiment that has shaped Filipinx American culture and self-understanding. As I mentioned above, the x helps me highlight these slippages as part of a more coherent archive of incoherence, wherein the epistemological borrowing of x in Filipinx from Latinx is actually part of an identifiable colonial continuum of experience. This spectrum of racial recognition and misrecognition is, I argue, a more satisfactory articulation of racial relatedness, rather than a simple misattribution or an example of overly enthusiastic borrowing. Because of its controversies, I want to reflect a bit more on the role of the x in constellating the alternative filiations and affinities that I attempt to mark with what has been pointed out to me as the capitalist pun of "dos x."

As I have written elsewhere, the very fact that "Filipino" or "Filipina" can be transmuted with the x in the first place demonstrates their origins as *Spanish* words.[21] They are ultimately colonial fabrications. They have indeed been resignified productively and endowed with different ethnonational meanings and affects. But such resignifications do not change the reality: the authenticity politics otherwise tied to more autochthonous uses of Filipino are compromised creations, latching ideations of autonomy to a cultural economy of coloniality that ultimately romanticizes their prescriptive usage. Or it might be more accurate to conclude that cultural economies of coloniality are reified through prescriptive uses of Filipino over Filipinx. Nationalist arguments against the use of Filipinx as an Americanized vanity project are tantamount to misguided self-enclosures that, quite frankly, fetishize Spanish morphological constructions of gender and race as the epistemological and ethnological currency of being Filipino or Filipina—or Latino and Latina, by the same token. I have studied Spanish for over two decades. I am a Filipino professor of Spanish well versed in the linguistic, cultural, and artistic developments of a very broad comparative and hemispheric American archive. I have taught over two thousand students the Spanish language. This experience has led me to be extremely suspicious and wholly unconvinced by arguments against use of the x where Filipino subjecthood is concerned.

Why anchor authentic uses and deployments of Filipino expression to colonial linguistic constructs that reproduce an ethnonational umbrella circumventing the ethnic diversity of a whole archipelago of cultural-linguistic expressions? And that do so in favor of a national rubric ultimately anchored in Manila cosmopolitanism and Hispanophilia? Here Hispanophilia is coextensive with homophobia and transphobia, which are the end result of the structure of identity empiricism that I wish to suspend for the purposes of this book. Despite all of this, I am not, in principle, against the use of "Filipino," as it is a useful and instructive shorthand in a world dominated by the political entity of the nation-state. Indeed, I use it, rather than Filipinx, to describe and identify myself. Moreover, subjective feelings of patriotic sentiment and filiation to a place in the world that we typically know of as "the Philippines" can be important signposts of collectivity. Nevertheless, *if these can be true*, that is, the sentimental and pedagogical use-value of "Filipino," then "Filipinx" can also do similar constellating work: through the satisfying mutation of colonial constructs of Spanish-origin words routed through a diaspora that is actually in more consistent contact with Latin America, the Borderlands, and the hemispheric Americas. If the Philippine national project (itself constructed through the desiderata conglomerated under the umbrella of the nation) wishes to hold up a Hispanic past as the hallmark of nationalism, then it needs to engage with all worlds summoned under and affected by the detritus of Spanish coloniality—including "Filipinx America."

Identity empiricism can short-circuit modes of solidarity that I argue are more evident, ironically, in moments of misrecognition. Like it or not, misrecognition racially embeds one's racialization within the destiny of another. Such moments construct one's self within the racial field that envelops another. I draw upon a few scholars in my own thinking about this queer sort of nonempirical dialectal recognition. Other philosophical renditions of recognition come into play that are productive to work alongside.

Perhaps the most widely recognized is that of Georg Wilhelm Friedrich Hegel in the master-slave dialectic. This famously appears in his foundational text *The Phenomenology of Spirit* (1807), in a chapter entitled "Lordship and Bondage."[22] Hegel observes that the self of self-consciousness has its origins in recognition. This is paradoxical, in the sense that the ontology of self-consciousness articulates the autonomy of selfhood in interdependence with cognizing the "self" of another from whom one requires recognition. In short, in order to be, you must yoke and command the recognition of another. Therefore, self is embedded in an economy of selves—an archipelago constituting a seemingly singular entity, rather than an island. As Hegel remarks quite stunningly:

> Self-consciousness has before it another self-consciousness; it has come outside itself. This has a double significance. First it has lost its own self, since it finds itself as an *other* being; secondly, it has thereby sublated that other, for it does not regard the other as essentially real, but sees its own self in the other.[23]

Echoing what we might associate with thinkers like W. E. B. Dubois, consciousness is always a double-consciousness.[24] Part of coming to the knowledge that one even has a self necessarily means, in Hegel's rendition, coming to terms with one's own otherness, thus "losing" the self as an evanescent construction. The response to this "self-otherment" is sublation with the comforting knowledge that one's essential being is bound up in the eventual annihilation of the other—ethically this is not a problem, because the other is not "essentially real." This will be familiar to those that confront permutations of the master-slave dialectic, in which the selves that believe themselves to be both autonomous and free engage in a struggle for recognition. The "master" submits the "bondsman" (sometimes translated as "slave") to his will in order to attain independence. In the course of this struggle, the master realizes that his independence is always mediated by the bondsman (for whom independence is annihilated), who, in turn, "labors upon it" (i.e., upon the independence of the master). What we can take away from Hegel's depiction that is useful for our understanding of recognition politics is that the self is a relation exterior to itself, which relies simultaneously on the prolonged fantasy of unobstructed autonomy and on categorical self-sameness. If the dialectic can be reasonably understood as the annihilation of the personhood and freedom of another in favor of the unitary freedom of self through a zero-sum game, I read this concept in contradistinction to philosophical conceptions of alterity and the recognition of fundamental difference.

Alterity, while not necessarily a philosophical foil to Hegel's master-slave thought experiment, furnishes clear differences to conceptions of freedom and autonomy that ensure insular subjectivities. Anchoring this project wholly to the Hegelian dialectic is insufficient, as it is clear that within the logic of the dialectic, not all can be free. In "alterity," rather than sublation, we have the antiphonal—a call and response that renders subjecthood within the script of relationality, rather than dialectology. Emmanuel Levinas distinguished between "need" and "desire" in this subjective economy.[25] Need fills a negation, and desire is positive attraction toward something other that is not yet possessed or needed. Desire is defined as the extra effort needed to be in communion with the other, not for purposes of domination or to subsume them into the narcissism of the self. Rather, this relation transpires through language and the total being and figuration of language: the uses and dispensations of language are meaningless without coming to terms with the linguistic registers of the other. You must be cognizant that an other has a perspective that is separate from yours, and exists autonomously from your interiority; to be in meaningful relation you must—to a certain degree—understand experience not simply through your imprimatur, but theirs as well. In my understanding, Levinas suggests that this fundamental recognition constitutes the idea of "infinity" (in opposition to "totality"). This Levinasian ethic indexes the infinity of being whose relation is linguistic, and gestures more toward an egalitarianism with the other or an other. Totality is the sphere of mastership maintaining a power arrangement in the master's favor. Infinity is the desire for more (potentially infinite) social relations where the self is decentered and the other is not simply an extension of the self and their obsessive dash for recognition, but rather they are their own entity, with their own desires and motivations. This framing of alterity (an ethical relation and intention toward the other) as language is key as one's selfhood, and is impossible to parameterize without its fundamental distinction from an *other*. In the realm of language, whose fundamental dispensation is to communicate ideas, one must negotiate a linguistic entity of self by coming to terms with the fundamental difference of the perspective of an other who may draw on similar linguistic registers or not. To meaningfully communicate, one must bridge this difference. This activity is agglutinative rather than dialectical. That is, it is relational rather than being about the other's subsumption into a unitary linguistic system.

It is interesting to understand Marx's materialism at the crossroads of Hegel and Levinas. In his critique of capitalism as a system of bourgeois capitalists owning the means of production and, essentially, the labor of the proletariat class, Marx is, famously, a follower of Hegel's dialectic. The proletarians are the bondsmen augmenting the wealth, power, and "self" of the capitalist class. Marx constructs an antidote for a system that alienates laborers from their own labor in order to exchange wages for commodity necessities. Laborers concord and then align their once myopic perceptions of their labors into a fuller account of the material conditions of their existence and their position within the political economy. We have come to know this as "class" or "class consciousness." As one might be able to intuit, we can observe the ways that the negative pull of historical materialism, propelled by an unequal distribution of resources and relation to the means of production, connect with notions of alterity. Nevertheless, it is not so much to affirm a fundamental difference between laborer A and laborer B. Instead, political consciousness as a unitary class of or kind of person recognizes sameness without the subjective dead end of self-sameness (or in Hegel's language, the sublation of the other).

Therefore, an insistence on identity empiricism necessarily pulls you away from that anxiety of misrecognition in order to be recognized for "who you really are" as a kind. As I have been arguing, moments of racial uncanny are productive of an ethic toward another that is necessarily not you, but with whom you share a bond of mutuality engineered by the socio-colonial environment that produces both of you as subjects of history—though such mutuality is not overdetermined by that environment. The suspension of the empirical opens up diagnostic pathways that allow for the meaningful assessment of the social, historical, and political architecture of the world that made misrecognition possible. Additionally, it potentiates the possibility of the coauthorship of modes of solidarity against the grain of the systemic dispossessions that engineer such moments of racial collapse of one into another. It is my hope that the rubric I am attempting to construct in which we can map potent moments of meaningful connection within landscapes of anxious misidentification will have an iterative effect, allowing others to trace alternative genealogies that intentionally intersect the discrete political traditions of separate groups demonstrating the ostensibility of that separation. In *Dos X*, the genealogy and mode of critique that I wish to construct uses Filipinx ambivalence and misrecognition as the heuristic for a cultural critique of racial capitalist ableism.

## Mapping the Book

The various case studies in this book aggregate the uncanny textures of racial dysphoria in several vital areas. Among them are the co-authorship of Filipinx and Latinx solidarity through bonds forged through error and misrecognition. Another theme that surfaces in these cultural texts is that of language. The modes of alternative or unexpected relation that emerge from the various bonds by error that I explore are often manifest in linguistic relations. As I elaborated above, racial error allows for shared colonial and linguistic registers to be more at the forefront. This takes up disability literary theory in a powerful way, as scholars like David T. Mitchell and Sharon L. Snyder have foundationally argued that the body is a linguistic relation that exceeds what the physical body encompasses.[26] As I explore throughout, language multivocalities emerge in property relations, the US able-body that manages them, and how whiteness becomes the rhetorical executor of such relations; the contours of racial drag, performativity, and impersonation; Filipinx and Latinx Spanishes as linguistic relations to colonialism; and the ways that cognitive disability reorients our attachments to migrant narratives.

The first chapter has an auspicious and unexpected beginning for this project on Filipinx and Latinx interracial intimacies: the American West. Specifically, this chapter homes in on what I suggest are the foundations of racial ableist capitalism that give historical and philosophical context for more contemporary subjects navigating its vicissitudes. The chapter also proposes an intervention into American studies by closely reading these ableist colonial genealogies in Frederick Jackson Turner's essay "The Significance of the Frontier in American History" (1894). The publication of this essay precedes by just a few years the US's occupation of the Philippines and demonstrates colonial logics that subtended American imperial power at the turn of the twentieth century. I thus approach the politics of ableism in the essay through a Filipinx studies lens. The structure of racial ableism and capitalism did not come from nowhere. And, while this chapter is not meant to be an exhaustive account of the origins of racial ableism, it does take up one of the foundational philosophical pillars of colonial ableism as a knowledge project. Additionally, because my project centers the politics and the aesthetics of racial drag, Turner's essay is indispensable in examining foundationally colonial iterations of this structure, whereby the pioneer transforms (into) the Indian.

Chapter Two analyzes the Filipinx American novel *American Son* by Brian Ascalon Roley. I might be tempted to categorize this 2001 novel as forming a part of a Filipinx-Chicanx cultural canon. *American Son* centers on the lives of two Filipinx American boys who engage in Mexican racial drag. One plays the part of Mexican in order to participate in illicit economies that might otherwise be foreclosed to him. Racialized drag becomes a way to navigate economic precarity and to attain a level of social mobility and security that does not assume assimilation into whiteness. The other "American son" is the queer first-person protagonist, who navigates his Asian racial queerness amidst an early 1990's Los Angeles in which pernicious discourses of criminalized ethnic masculinities circulate. Through close reading, I argue that the encounter of effeminate Asian American subjects with criminalized ethnic Mexican masculinities in a post-riot Los Angeles landscape positions the queerness of racial ambiguity as a critique of racial capitalism and borderization. I also read Roley's Filipinx-Chicanx novel as an invitation to explore how the Asian houseboy trope and the Mexican migrant domestic worker—and their various interactions—aid us in re-genealogizing the US-Mexican borderscape as a transpacific encounter attentive to how race, gender, and sexuality shape political economy and its representations. In making this critique, the analysis focuses on the appearance of Filipinx Spanglish as an unexpected variety of what Gloria Anzaldúa has called "deficient Spanish" of the US-Mexico Borderlands, tacitly highlighting a connection to the disabling realities of the racialized political realities of the border.

Chapter Three renews the analysis of racial drag through the optic of racial misrecognition and error experienced by the undocumented Filipinx American immigration advocate Jose Antonio Vargas. I analyze various statements made by Vargas on being misclassified or categorized as Mexican, given the racial contours of the US immigration debate in which he found himself a prominent lightning rod and mouthpiece following the publication of his 2018 memoir *Dear America: Notes of an*

*Undocumented Citizen*. I offer analysis of these autobiographical moments of racial misrecognition that are charted in Vargas's disclosure of his legal status as undocumented. I argue that these instances, taken together, offer rich insights on the ways in which we can utilize cultural production and politics to map the coordinates of a more unified Latinx and Filipinx studies whose connections are partly articulated through subtended yet shared histories of colonial encounter. These colonialisms are those of Spain and the United States, whose intersecting realities in many of the nations of the world are also bound profoundly together in the diasporic populations of the Philippines and Latin America in the United States. I demonstrate that comparative ethnic studies must attend closely to comparative empire. Additionally, it shows that the constellation work of the dos x of Latinx and Filipinx studies potentiates these fields as an anti-imperial co-formation that captures an understanding of the politics of race within a truly global matrix.

Further elaborating the thematic of language and translation, Chapter Four builds a close-reading analysis of the American television series *Undone*. The show artfully explores the "elastic nature of reality" through the perspective of its Mexican American deaf and schizophrenic protagonist, Alma Winograd-Díaz. Alma navigates a surreal rotoscoped transition from deaf to hearing, while also experiencing the onset of symptoms consistent with schizophrenia. The show's plot centers on investigating the events surrounding her father's death when she was a child, while also coming to understand the nature of her father's neuroscientific research on schizophrenia. *Undone* establishes Alma's experience of both her deafness and neurodivergence as bound up with an exploration of her racial mestiza identity. Moreover, the nonlinear and disjointed ways that she explores this identity open up the limited geographies through which Mexican migrant identity is typically understood. I argue that this opens comparative pathways that connect Latinx and Asian American migrant subjectivities across language, space, and time, demonstrating that disability enhances a comparative ethnic studies analysis, materializing through what I call a "mad migrant imaginary," to extend Alicia Schmidt Camacho's brilliant concept. This imaginary is comparative and considers the racial, colonial, linguistic, and political environments in which ableism is situated—with particular attention to the US-Mexico Borderlands. In doing so, such a framework considers colonial antecedents to the US nation-state, which is a site of struggle for accommodation for disabled people, while simultaneously problematizing the state's centrality as a settler formation in disability analysis. My general claim is that, without centering the racial-colonial, a disability analysis risks propounding the effects of the colonial and its inherent disabling effects. I also seek to attend to the ways that disability—which analytically tracks the distribution of vulnerability across difference—is vital for a comparative racial analysis of dispossession. I want to make it clear that disability analysis benefits greatly from racial analysis, and that disability stands to enrich a critique of racism. I avoid positioning disability as a transcendent mode of difference that phases out race by implicitly assuming its parochial status for understanding the body and its differences. Instead, I suggest that attending to the generalized imposition of disablement across communities explicitly engages with the ways that race is a logic that rationalizes, promotes, and politically sanctions disablement.

# 1 | Ability as Property
## *On the Frontier Prosthesis and Colonial Drag*

### The Drag of the Colonial

This book begins perhaps unexpectedly in the American West. Frederick Jackson Turner, the subject of study of this chapter, is one of the first theorists of one of the central phenomena that preoccupies this book: the colonial technology of racial drag. While *Dos X* attends to contemporary manifestations of reactive forms of conscripted racial drag, it is important to recognize a colonial genealogy of racial performativity that shapes the psychic experience of threshold subjectivity. As I stated in the introduction, the racial misrecognitive is a unique form of epistemic disclosure that prompts, to my mind, the construction of diagnostic criteria to understand the constellation of bodies, affects, and political discourse that occasion racial misrecognition in the first place. As I argued in the presentation of the philosophical framework that undergirds this project, "Misrecognition is a unique kind of experience, in the sense of it indexing a heightened awareness of yourself as a particular subject of history *and* how you are an object of the multiplicities of stories—as disaggregated as they may be—via the gaze of another." So now I attempt to render a history of the present by reverse engineering the moment of misrecognition in order to understand its etiologies. This has led me to the American West, to the march of American progressive masculinity across the Borderlands, and to the white heteronormative homestead as romantically presented by US historian Frederick Jackson Turner. The misrecognitive diasporas that threshold and braid together Filipinx and Latinx identities must confront the settler colonial reality of Indigenous annihilative displacement and Black enslavement. It is these realities that shape the contours of racial capitalism and colonial ableism that set the stage for the vertiginous experience of racial dysphoria. As the reader will see in the pages that follow, Turner was preoccupied with the potentially fragile ability of the brittle European body. In order for it to be rehabilitated, this body had to become American. The frontier wilds of what would become appropriated and integrated as the western United States were the colonial laboratory where this transformation would occur—delineating racial prostheses that endowed the Americanized body with a unique racial ability appropriated from the Indian. Thus, American identity itself is a durable and protracted form of racial drag that manifests disablement in others.

## Manifest Disablement

In this chapter I examine permutations of the colonial discourse of Manifest Destiny to understand the ways that colonial capitalist expansion deployed settler colonialism and antiblackness to augment white property. This multivalent mode of comparative and parallel racial dispossession has been explored by a number of scholars in the fields of critical race theory and critical ethnic studies.[1] The outgrowth of US colonialism through westward expansion across the continental United States transformed land and persons into property by racially marking bodies that were to be utilized as resources. The geopolitics of this expansion, the Borderlands of colonial encounter, and the American frontier consolidated whiteness as a legal, political, and racial category of property and propertied liberal subjecthood.[2] That is, the law transformed whiteness into legal property to be protected from others, and constitutively produced a liberal subject that could own properties, lands, and people as a contract-wielding citizen.[3] This is a central theoretical discourse animating much conversation, inquiry, scholarship, and activism destabilizing what has been called the possessive investment in whiteness.[4]

I depart from and add to these critical ethnic studies conversations by way of a genealogical engagement with a foundational framework in American studies: Frederick Jackson Turner's "frontier thesis." In engaging with Turner's essay "The Significance of the Frontier in American History" (1894), which auspiciously heralded the advent of American imperialism in the twentieth century, I hone in on the property logics of whiteness as they were articulated in the aftermath of the Civil War, during Reconstruction, and within the incipient shadow of US transpacific expansionism.[5] Turner's frontier holds particular importance in the development of American Progressivist discourses that postulated the rehabilitation of colonized subjects as an effect of their dispossession.[6]

Such is the case with the Progressivist discourse of "Benevolent Assimilation," which rationalized imperial conquest of the Philippines, Guam, Puerto Rico, and Cuba following the Spanish-American War (1898).[7] "Benevolent" empire is a logic whose antecedents can be located in the Turnerian frontier. The Caribbean and the Pacific were the "new frontiers" after the traditional frontier in the western United States had been won—a historical and epochal shift that is canonized for us by Turner's founding of the project of American history as a scholarly endeavor at the State Historical Society of Wisconsin in the late nineteenth century.[8] The proximity of Turner's thesis with these imperial developments is a springboard for engaging the idea of the American frontier in a global context. What is presented in his paper is transpacific in thought and method.[9] Thus, I consider my critique of the so-called "frontier thesis" as a contribution to Filipinx American studies, and believe it potentiates this field's critical contributions to crip theory. As a Filipinx American critic, I reverse engineer the "benevolent" colonization of the Philippines, migrating back to Turner's frontier to understand the logics of racial dispossession and its "curative violences"—to invoke a disability framework imagined by Eunjung Kim.[10] In tow with the late nineteenth- and early twentieth-century ideological imagination that the human being and body could be perfected through reform, I see the intersection of geopolitical expansion, rehabilitation, and racial capitalist dispossession as an "archive of liberalism" in which the analysis of disability finds a telling racialized colonial genealogy.[11]

Recent scholarship in disability studies has attempted to make more explicit connections between colonialism, race, and disability as part of an effort to articulate what Jina Kim and Sami Schalk have provocatively called a "crip-of-color critique."[12] Part of this work has reflected on the ways that oppressive forces like colonialism or racism have caused literal impairments, as well as the ways that their logics influence political systems that impair capacity. Colonial systems disable their populations in order to subjugate them by making them "available for injury."[13] Worth noting is that, as argued in the pioneering work of scholar and disability activist Mike Oliver, "impairment" and "disability" are typically distinguished from one another in disability studies.[14] Impairment is the literal description of the disabled body that furnishes a difference from the norm. Disability is the social arrangement and power structure that order bodies that may or may not be medically understood to be impaired. However, where race is concerned, this binary definition distinguishing the impaired material body from discursive disability is not always the most instructive.

I add to the urgent and important calls of opening up disability analysis, which has traditionally been a Eurocentric and "white" field, to consider other global or postcolonial contexts that tell alternative stories about the body.[15] Where these interventions get complicated is in those instances where disability might not be exclusively about the phenomenological experience or fact of disability, but rather when certain colonial and racial discourses systematize disablement. Indeed, rather than disability being a transhistorical "fact" about the human body, what constitutes it is shaped by the social, historical, and political environment. In invoking the term disablement, I attempt to get at the discursive reality of disability that certainly inhabits the body, but also exceeds its boundaries. One might be physically able-bodied but live under a colonial system structured by privations that diminish human flourishing. For instance, in postcolonial studies, while literal physical violence is never minimized, the epistemic or discursive violence of colonialism is just as deleterious.[16] Colonial reality influences the ways in which we have historically understood racial fitness for political sovereignty and the perceived mental capacities required to effectively carry out the responsibilities of liberalism.[17] The proliferation of scientific racism in the nineteenth and twentieth centuries is another case in point. Fields like phrenology, craniology, and ethnology were all part of systems of knowledge production measuring (sometimes literally as a function of volume) the cognitive capacity of supposedly lesser races.[18] These scientific logics disabled discursively "inferior" races even if they were not disabled in fact. In the same ways that political systems might be colonially structured even if they are not literal colonialism,[19] the logic of "disability" persists irrespective of the presence of an impaired body that would produce anxiety in the able-bodied person that would appraise it.[20] These more epistemological injuries shape ideas around the body and predispose it to particular harms, thus constituting an important avenue of study for disability theorists. The discursivity of violence in this sense speaks to the discursivity of disability. In this chapter, I understand race as a mode through which disability attains definitional parameters. To study race is to inevitably study disability. Similarly, engaging disability as a form of extra-normative embodiment unavoidably means paying attention to how race is enmeshed with the human body.

Aligned with this theoretical trajectory of combining race critique with disability analysis, I propose that we crip the frontier thesis. "Crip" is a disability analytic that enumerates the ways that institutions, ideologies, and violence shape our ideas of normative embodiment.[21] Much like queer theory is a critique of normativity, crip theory similarly demonstrates how the able-body and -mind are epistemologically and ontologically assumed in the ways we structure society, history, and scholarly inquiry.[22] Disability is not a compelling dimension of difference, robustly considered in intersectional models of analysis, because we do not wish to be disabled.[23] It is a maligned form of embodiment to be avoided, shunned, or rehabilitated—a "master trope of disqualification."[24] However, it is through a disability analysis that I strive to show that it is not only a possessive investment in whiteness that operationalized colonial property logics in US Empire, but also a possessive investment in a uniquely racialized American ability forged in the colonial frontier. Not only did a white American "bodymind" emerge as an enlightened steward of lands that he could judiciously (and legally) possess, but the legal franchise of property also bore out a masculinist pioneer body that adroitly traversed land, forded rivers, and climbed mountains.[25] White property envisaged a white able-body that could competently cross into the frontier, and a rational mind that could expertly develop such "ownerless" lands. Moreover, the project of territorial development requires robust physical capacities in order to perform the labors of working the land. The rational mind and the physical body are not separate entities, but profoundly interconnected. The able-mind is the vessel of capitalist ideology actualized by the work of an able-body—a body that is coded as white. Colonial property is produced through the legal regime of propertied whiteness; nevertheless, I claim that white property is managed by a liberal mind and a pioneer body—both crystallized through an unprecedented American racial ability.

Crip and queer critique align in revealing the ableist dimensions of US imperialism—dimensions that I theorize as "manifest disablement." Manifest disablement necessitates two interconnected forms of coloniality. The first is the dispossession of the ability of non-white bodies to be owners or sovereign agents in relation to land, which augments the physical and mental ability of the white able-body.[26] The second is the presumptive heteronormativity of colonial property logics. These taken together define "manifest disablement" as a form of colonial ableism that productively organizes the development of land through the implantation of the heteronormative homestead. As we will see on the granular level in Turner's frontier thesis, the able-bodied pioneer is also significantly and tediously heterosexual; the pioneer is the rugged head of the heteronuclear household built on the lands that he surveyed—lands that he cultivates to further the reproduction of a heteronormative racial state. We can identify what crip theorist Robert McRuer calls the heterosexuality of "compulsory able-bodiedness" within white supremacist property logics.[27] Nevertheless, the constitutive reality of propertied ableism is the manifestation of disablement in colonial others, and it thus expresses the political discourse of Manifest Destiny as an intractable desire for a white able-body. The desire for native land as property and Black bodies as chattel entrenches within imperial logics an ideology of ableism. American frontier logics are a historical arena in which these intersections of race, property, and body are elaborated. If ableism is a colonial logic that manifests the frontier, then it seems logical that to shore up the parameters of the able-body implicates the production of disability as a racialized logic of dispossession. In short, disability is a colonial logic of capitalist dispossession. Following David Harvey's definition of capitalism as accumulation via dispossession, I propose not only that the colonial bodymind accumulates land and property via dispossession, but also that, in the project of racial capitalism, the white able-bodied property owner accumulates ability via racialized disablement.[28] This ableist accumulation is manifest disablement. There are bodies that are able to own and cultivate land, and there are bodies that are unfit to hold deeds to property or are only fit to be property themselves. The habilitation of a white imperial body constitutively instantiates the disablement of Indigenous and Black peoples, whose exclusion from the regimes of white property marks their exclusion from American normative ability.

In short, property is ability manifest. Much like whiteness, ability discursively functions as a form of property. The frontier disables the racially dispossessed in order to augment white ability as a function of colonial property relations. Both the augmentation of white property and the proliferation of white property logics as normative contractual relations manifested themselves through an ideology of ableism. US civilization is built as much upon the idea of an able-body as it is built on the ideal of a white, male body. In other words, the US American who conquered the frontier needs to be white, male, straight, *and* able. As I elaborated above, the expansion and assumption of property through territorial conquest was reliant on the mythos of a white able-bodied male pioneer who could cross and tame the wild nature of the frontier. The frontier, as Turner would argue, was the singularly most important variable preventing American identity from simply being an extension of European institutions and culture. While various European countries were certainly invested in the global construction of extractive franchise colonies, they did not have the cultural and geographic imposition of a frontier. Turner reasoned that this imposition and (literal) horizon of desire were unique to the American experience.

## THE FRONTIER PROSTHESIS

Legal theorist Cheryl I. Harris explores how "economic hegemony over Black and Native American peoples" demonstrates the ways that property and race are conceptually inextricable. Specifically, whiteness is a form of property whose definitional borders were drawn around "a right to exclude." I am interested in this "conceptual nucleus" that Harris theorizes, in which whiteness and property co-constitute each other through the economic privations exacted on populations excluded from whiteness through the dispossession of land, as was the case with Indians, and the transformation of human beings into property, as was the case with enslaved Africans.[29] Excluding people of color from whiteness rationalizes the argument that whiteness historically developed as a form of property. To wit, Harris writes:

> The origins of property rights in the United States are rooted in racial domination. Even in the early years of the country, it was not the concept of race alone that operated to oppress Blacks and Indians; rather, it was the interaction between conceptions of race and property that played a critical role in establishing and maintaining racial and economic subordination.
>
> The hyperextraction of Black labor was accomplished by treating Black people as objects of property. Race and property were thus conflated by establishing a form of property contingent on race—only Blacks were subjugated as slaves and treated as property. Similarly, the conquest, removal, and extermination of Native American life and culture were ratified by conferring and acknowledging the property rights of whites in Native American land. Only white possession and occupation of land was validated and therefore privileged as a basis for property rights. These distinct forms of exploitation each contributed in varying ways to the construction of whiteness as property.[30]

In other words, whiteness came to stand in for liberal personhood, legally recognized as a property of white people.[31] Blackness connoted an annihilation of such personhood, and thus whiteness constituted a "shield from slavery."[32] Blackness then ontologically meant enslaveability. The political-economic system of slavery

> linked the privilege of whites to the subordination of Blacks through a legal regime that attempted the conversion of Blacks into objects of

> property. Similarly, the settlement and seizure of Native American land supported white privilege through a system of property rights in land in which the "race" of the Native Americans rendered their first possession rights invisible and justified conquest. This racist formulation embedded the fact of white privilege into the very definition of property.[33]

Thus, whiteness as a conceptual legal definition, which only whites possess, "is valuable and is property."[34]

Whiteness entitled white people to land and chattel. Critical ethnic studies scholar Iyko Day has similarly argued that these forms of dispossession worked in tandem to augment white property.[35]

While Day makes a similar argument to Harris, it is not predicated exclusively on the legal precedents shaping propertied whiteness. Instead (and in addition), she significantly does work to reconcile seemingly incommensurate theoretical interventions in Afropessimism and settler colonial studies. A conservative version of the latter argues that, irrespective of involuntary migration history, the presence of non-natives problematically annihilates what Patrick Wolfe calls "native alternatives."[36] In other words, even the descendants of slaves further the project of settler colonialism. While this is a challenging critique—which, as Day argues, underestimates the impact of voluntary versus involuntary migrations—what I think is useful is the emphasis on settler coloniality being an effect of structure rather than siloed to intent. Afropessimist thought as it is characterized by Day, on the other hand, seeks to understand Blackness as the foundational negation of humanity—an ontology that supersedes and fundamentally structures all other forms of dehumanization. While native genocide is certainly a crucial history not to be underestimated, even native identity would fit in a white supremacist power structure, conferring marginal privileges that would never be available to Black people. Some corroborating empirical evidence can be found in work by historian Tiya Miles.[37] Although problematic racialized labor relations have certainly had deleterious impacts on many communities, it seems historically sound to argue that antiblackness has served a foundational role in organizing labor in relation to race. Foundational Latin American theorists of mestizaje, for instance, have clarified that American independence and nation-building (perhaps including the United States) possess an understated link to transatlantic slavery, even as this theory of racial hybridity is understood to incorporate indigeneity into national identity. Many theorists have established that this incorporation reifies antiblackness.[38] Although distinct from a US American milieu, indigenous incorporation partially as a function of antiblackness is not too far off of what the Turnerian frontier attempts.

The formation of the US American racial state was predicated, as Harris and Day have explicated, on the consolidation of whiteness as a form of property and also, I would add, on the integration of whiteness into the idealized form of the able-bodied pioneer. In a moment where Harris clearly articulates her main argument, I detect a discursive shift into thinking through the legal discourse of propertied whiteness and its attendant articulation to a physical body assumed to be able:

> Whiteness defined the legal status of a person as slave or free. White identity conferred tangible and economically valuable benefits and was jealously guarded as a valued possession, allowed only to those who met a strict standard of proof. Whiteness—the right to white identity as embraced by the law—is property if by property one means all of a person's legal rights . . . property is the delegation of sovereign power . . . Indian custom was obliterated by force and replaced with the regimes of common law that embodied the customs of the conquerors. The assumption of American law as it related to Native Americans was that conquest *did* give rise to sovereignty. Indians experienced the property laws of the colonizers and the emergent American nation as acts of violence perpetuated by the exercise of power and ratified through the rule of law. At the same time, these laws were perceived as custom and "common sense" by the colonizers. The Founders, for instance [,] so thoroughly embraced Lockean labor theory as the basis for the right of acquisition because it affirmed the right of the New World settlers to settle on and acquire the frontier. It confirmed and ratified their experience.[39]

I want to suggest through an engagement with Harris's foundational essay that white property is the realm in which race and disability intersect politically and empirically. Also, disability functions as the dividing line between property and dispossession. Above, Harris defines for us the ways that property is a social relation that is produced through "a whole host of intangibles that are the product of labor, time, and creativity."[40] Harris's invocation of the "frontier" in the above passage demonstrates the extent to which "Lockean" understandings of labor reify whiteness into property as a function of work. If work and socially necessary labor time are foundational realities for white property, labor definitively implicates a physical body that can satisfactorily perform the work of property. The transformation of the wild frontier into ordered property evokes a tangible white body that can enjoy the "intangibles" of his labor. Turner's foundational frontier thesis introduces a complication to this able-bodied laborer above that potentially contravenes the purity of whiteness that seems operative in Harris's theory. In a particularly evocative part of Turner's essay, he describes the body that physically crosses into frontier lands:

> [The frontier] finds him (the American pioneer) a European in dress, industries, tools, modes of travel, and thought. It takes him from the railroad car and puts him in the birch canoe. It strips off the garments of civilization and arrays him in the hunting shirt and the moccasin. It puts him in the log cabin of the Cherokee and Iroquois and runs an Indian palisade around him. Before long he has gone to planting Indian corn and plowing with a sharp stick, he shouts the war cry and takes the scalp in orthodox Indian fashion. In short, at the frontier the environment is at first too strong for the man. He must accept the conditions which it furnishes, or perish, and so he fits himself into the Indian clearings and follows the Indian trails.[41]

This passage points to one of the main political tensions at the heart of Turner's intellectual project of founding what today would be called "American studies." Was America its own distinct culture and entity with its own separate history, or was it merely an extension of European culture and institutions? Turner's answer lies in the ways that the American pioneer is arrayed in "the hunting shirt and the moccasin" and finds himself dwelling in the "log cabin of the Cherokee and Iroquois."[42] This description of the American pioneer transforming himself into an Indian demonstrates that the most important factor that differentiated "European . . . thought" from that of America was the frontier. The frontier's harsh conditions, which are "at first too strong for the man," showed that the completely white European was not equipped to handle the rough conditions of frontier life. He must adopt the position of—and racially transform himself into—a "savage" to attain the capacities that are requisite to "[plant] Indian corn" and "[plow] with a sharp stick." He can then thrive, rather than "perish," as he "follows the Indian trails." Unlike the slave that performs labors on behalf of the white capitalist cultivating and proliferating "cotton culture," as Turner calls it, here a peculiar form of racial drag materializes in which the white body does and does not perform its own work. Is this body Indian or white? Both? It is clear from Turner's writing that this "part-Indian" pioneer is cultivating lands that he will own—the lands are ownerless because they lack this cultivation and are thus "primitive," requiring much needed development via colonial capitalism. His whiteness, in contradistinction to the Indian whose land claims are inoculated, grants him a legal status as property owner. Nevertheless, his European civilization is also inadequate to the physical tasks that are required to navigate the frontier or to perform the creative labors required to transform savage lands into developed US American homesteads.

Disability studies scholars David T. Mitchell and Sharon L. Snyder have analyzed the ways that literary and expressive cultures, particularly the novel, facilitate the development of protagonists through an ideology of ableism. Cultural and literary representation are not benign symbolism, but actively shape the discourse through which bodies are imagined and are, indeed, made to signify. Importantly, for them, "the body is first and foremost a linguistic relation which cannot be natural or average . . . a theoretical premise from which all bodies must, by definition, fall short."[43] The body is an abstraction against which the material body fails to measure up. The discrepancy between the materiality and the idealization of the body produces an anxiety managed through the demonization of disability. The result is a dimension of difference that un-abstracts the body in ways that are too uncomfortable for Western society's trenchant belief in individualism, independence, and sovereignty—domains of liberalism that are often secured through the dispossession of others. As Mitchell and Snyder observe, in much of the canon of Western Anglophone literature, in order to shore up the narrative anxiety around the potential impairments that should never affect the protagonist (who must be normative), "narrative prosthesis" is deployed to both manage bodily anxiety and ensure an illusory corporeal wholeness. They write that a "body deemed lacking, unfunctional, or inappropriately functional needs compensation, and a prosthesis helps to affect this end." Impairments, disabilities, or other deviations from ideal embodiments "extract one from a social norm or average of bodies and their corresponding social expectations."[44] A "prosthetic device" is articulated in narrative to bear the burden of the physical and cognitive disabilities, which the protagonist overcomes, supersedes, or even rehabilitates to find bodily and narrative wholeness. Functionally, the protagonist with whom the reader identifies holds the vaunted corporeal normativity that is idealized and desired, while a secondary character suffers the social exclusions of disability—this character is the prosthetic ensuring the wholeness, fitness, and desirability of able-bodied protagonism, thus "return[ing] the body to the invisible status of normative essence."[45]

In the above passage, the white European body, by Turner's own admission, is impaired by the frontier. He must be "stripped of the garments of [European] civilization." This body requires the body of the Indian to secure a wholeness and able-bodied acumen necessary to conquer the frontier, thus transforming it into property that can be legally owned by him because of his propertied whiteness. The Indian is transformed into a prosthetic device for the pioneer protagonist of American history. This idea tracks with the settler colonial theory of "elimination" in which, as Patrick Wolfe has argued, the complete eradication of the Indian counterintuitively contravenes the assertion of settler sovereignty. Wolfe argues that

> the erasure of indigeneity conflicts with the assertation of settler nationalism. On the one hand, settler society required the practical elimination of the natives in order to establish itself on their territory. On the symbolic level, however, settler society subsequently sought to recuperate indigeneity in order to express its difference—and, accordingly, its independence from the mother country.[46]

Thus the Indian palimpsestically remains as a phantasmal presence in white settler society—never completely eradicated, but not completely or corporeally present, either. In calling this a "logic of elimination," Wolfe draws a contrast with full-blown genocide—although elimination and genocide serve as corollary logics. The Indian is differentially included in settler society through the preservation of a native culture in the form of symbolism and iconography, as well as folktales not unlike the one of the heroic pioneer presented to us by Turner. The white pioneer body, with its native prosthesis aiding the conqueror's passage through savage "Indian palisades," confirms the insight that "settler colonialism does not simply replace native society *tout court*. Rather, the process of replacement maintains the refractory imprint of the native counter-claim."[47] The curiosity that the frontier inspired in American backwoodsmen was possessed and actualized by a dexterous Indian body. Settler independence and ingenuity require a surreptitious rehabilitation of an unfit European body through the crip presence of an Indian prosthesis.

This backwoodsman is the product of what I call Turner's "frontier prosthesis." Drawing on the analysis above clarifies that manifest disablement describes the racial process of capitalist dispossession through which an able-body obtains ownership through the social contract of property. The transformation of Indian land into American property produces robust ability for the pioneer, and disables through dispossession the native who is affixed as a prosthetic device. Rather than the Indian being placed into the American landscape (as has been suggested by some), the socio-political environment of the frontier occasions a corporeal sublimation of the Indian as a physical capacity to be deployed by a white body.[48] Reading through this framework, "The Significance of the Frontier in American History" constructs an American manly identity through the proliferation of an ideology of ability.[49] Disability theorist Tobin Siebers defined an "ideology of ability" as "at its simplest the preference for able-bodiedness."[50] It also "defines the baseline by which humanness is determined, setting the measure of body and mind that gives or denies human status to individual persons."[51] Importantly, one of Siebers's greatest insights is that the disabled body becomes the invisible center around which our judgment of human ability and bodily preference revolve. Ableism then is a liberal formulation that simultaneously invisibilizes the body as an ideological apparatus in itself and consolidates the unstated desire for its perfectibility. I extend Siebers's explication to claim that US Empire is a historical articulation of ableism in its colonial desire for the perfectibility of the American body. A white able-body is imagined figuratively as physically capable of crossing frontier-land, adroitly traversing hostile terrain, and manipulating the environment to suit his needs.

Following the theoretical conversation on white property elaborated by scholars like Harris and Day, it is important to also emphasize the ways that this habilitation of the white body through the elimination of the Indian—what I call the "frontier prosthesis" above—works in tandem with the political economy of slavery. I claim that the way that the frontier prosthesis inculcates the imprint of native culture into white property is through the reification of Black slaves *as property*. Teleologically, the "frontier" is overdetermined in Turner's formulation as the singularly most important historical variable, disarticulated from the slavocracy that gave the movement west its initial impetus. The frontier eclipses all other political and economic considerations, particularly with regard to the "slavery question":

> The legislation which most developed the powers of the national government, and played the largest part in its activity, was conditioned on the frontier. Writers have discussed the subjects of tariff, land, and internal improvement, as subsidiary to the slavery question. But when American history comes to be rightly viewed it will be seen that the slavery question

is an incident. In the period from the end of the first half of the present century to the close of the Civil War slavery rose to primary, but far from exclusive, importance.[52]

The question of slavery as the element that marked the United States' political environment in the mid-nineteenth century is represented as an obstacle that causes misunderstanding of the true nature of American identity. Therefore, according to Turner, the American frontier "as a field for the serious study of the economist and the historian . . . has been neglected."[53] The American frontier perhaps marks one of the earliest historiographical attempts to entrench whiteness and imperial capitalism by amplifying the curious historical absence of Blackness. In a similar turn characteristic of the "eliminatory logic" of settler colonialism, the question of slavery is likewise overshadowed by the frontier. I suggest that the very prosthetic transformation in which the white able-body sublimates his desire for the Native body's capacities finds its underlying mode of production in the equally invisibilized labor of the Black body.

In a stunning display of transposition, the white American nuclear family and the attendant gendered divisions of labor constitutive of rugged pioneer life eclipse the political economic realities of the "slavery question." The American bodies that perform and adhere to the gendered labor divisions of American heteronormativity are affixed with native prostheses. The eclipsing of the native prosthesis and slavery reifies the pioneer able-body as the seductive symbology of the historiographic frontier. White heteronormativity crystallizes the unique American character of the family as a cornerstone of civilization even though "Germanic germs" find possible contamination due to contact with "savage" Indian tribes. As we will see, Indian identity and land claims are used to minimize the importance of slavery to the American political economy. A previous rupture and crisis in US racial capitalism activated by the Civil War is resolved through the in-vogue frontier naturalism of a Great West, hard-won through various Indian Wars.[54] Nevertheless, the gendered work of the heteronormative frontier family constitutes colonial capitalist labors surreptitiously scaffolded by Black bodies.

## Heteronormative Homestead

Literary scholar Amy Kaplan's essay "Manifest Domesticity" was one of the formative theoretical interventions into what would be consolidated as studies of US empire.[55] This work introduced a key feminist theoretical lens to the critique of US imperialism. Despite the undertheorization of Kaplan's particular intervention, she nevertheless demonstrated how empire brings with it clear heteronormative logics, which gain power through colonial racism. In this section, I aim to demonstrate that the crux of racism and heteronormativity lie within ableist property relations as well. A critique of the colonial logics of property is incomplete without a thorough consideration of the normative straightness of the able-bodied pioneer. I claim that the frontier prosthesis not only shaped a colonial "normate" body in the American imaginary, but also envisioned that body emplotted on a heteronormative homestead—itself constructed through gendered divisions of labor.[56] Kaplan posed fundamental questions regarding the supposed separation of the US domestic sphere from its territorial expansions abroad. Indeed, the "out there" of US foreign policy and the "right here" of US domestic politics exist in a dialectical relationship.

Manifest Destiny wasn't just racist. It was heteronormative. Women's domestic labors were a foundational aspect of US empire building. The ideology of separate spheres cleaving the domestic space of women's work from the male public space of political discourse in the early to mid-nineteenth century "contributed to creating an American Empire by imagining the nation as a home at a time when its geopolitical borders were expanding rapidly through violent confrontations with Indians, Mexicans, and European empires."[57] Later in the essay Kaplan provocatively argues that "Women's work at home . . . performs two interdependent forms of national labor; it forges the bonds of internal unity while impelling the nation outward to encompass the globe."[58] In short, two interdependent manifestations must converge for the success of the US imperial project—which is manifest in domesticity as well as in destiny. Thus, identifying what is foreign to American culture is indissociable from the gendered domestic work of creating the American home. The domestic space—specifically, the white American home—of US Empire turns on the cultural distillation of a sex-gender system rooted in racial ideology. Recall that Turner's pioneer becomes the Indian savage that he dispossesses, appropriating the Indian's robust capacities that are not germane to European embodiment. Nevertheless, the pioneer does not lose his constitutive relationship to propertied whiteness. The discourse of manifest domesticity and manifest disablement intertwine in the perpetuation of colonial property as a heteronormative institution.

I suggest that what stabilizes the connection of property to whiteness in the frontier is a colonial form of heteronormativity. This is particularly evident in Turner's extended citation of John Mason Peck's *A New Guide to the American West* (1837), which described progressive stages of settlement by three different kinds of settlers, thus giving the reader a taxonomy of pioneers. This taxonomy is unfolded through a description of a heteronormative family dynamic. The initial—indeed, chronologically first—class of settlers is particularly illuminating with regard to the question of imperial domesticity. The West is won not only by the rugged individualism of the American pioneer, but also by the propagation of the American family as a political economic rationality:

> Generally, in all the western settlements, three classes, like the waves of the ocean, have rolled one after the other. First comes the pioneer, who depends for *the subsistence of his family* chiefly upon the natural growth of vegetation, called the "range," and the proceeds of hunting. His implements of agriculture are rude, chiefly of his own make, and his efforts directed mainly to a crop of corn and a "truck patch." The last is a rude garden for growing cabbage, beans, corn for roasting ears, cucumbers, and potatoes. A log cabin, and, occasionally, a stable and corn-crib, and a field of a dozen acres, the timber girdled or 'deadened' and fenced, are enough for his occupancy. It is quite immaterial whether he ever becomes the owner of the soil. He is the occupant for the time being, pays no rent, and feels as independent as the "lord of the manor." With a horse, cow, and one or two breeders of swine, he strikes into the woods with his family, and becomes the founder of a new country, or perhaps state. He builds his cabin, gathers around him a few other families of similar tastes and habits, and occupies till the range is somewhat subdued, and hunting a little precarious, or, which is more frequently the case, till the neighbors crowd around, roads, bridges, and fields annoy him, and he lacks elbow room. The preemption law enables him to dispose of his cabin and cornfield to the next class of emigrants . . . [59]

In Turner's essay the primitive frontier family does not fully connote barbarity, but rather a naturalization of heteronormativity as the civilizing ethos central to pioneer life. While his implements for cultivation are "rude" and it is "immaterial whether he ever becomes the owner of the soil," he, his family, and the "other families of similar tastes and habits" ready the range for "the next class of emigrants." In Turner's taxonomy, the rudeness of the initial wave paves the way for higher successive forms of civilization with encroaching waves of immigration. What is striking is the multiple mentions of the family as the node around which migration, development, and cultivation revolve. While earlier in the essay, Turner portrays an odd racial drag of the white pioneer prosthetically-enhanced as Indian that might connote an abdication of civilization, the author goes to great citational effort to show that such racial performativity as a "savage" does not make the pioneer an atavistic subject. Rather, the pioneer is the instrument of colonial development who maintains his civilization because of his dedication to the American family. Put succinctly, heteronormativity is what shields the frontiersman and his family from the savagery of their return to the state of nature. Heteronormativity is also the ideological matrix through which the white able-body owns its own labor and thus also owns the land subjected to the development of that labor. And, indeed, such imperial norming is that which renders the white body self-same rather than unrecognizably Indian—a racial coherence fundamental to the ableist logics of property. The heteronormative family living on the colonial homestead offers the much-needed civilizational anchor that the pioneer might lose after "going native." In a similar way that whiteness serves as a shield from enslaveability, as argued by Harris and Day, heteronormativity serves as a shield from racial primitivism, even as such normativity facilitates the extraction of the vaunted physical abilities of the native who must be disappeared. The heteronormative family and property relations seemingly ensure the appropriation of native culture repackaged as rugged frontier life. It is this family unit that makes the body and the labors that the able-bodied pioneer performs also forms of white property. Heteronormativity and the institution of the family are what facilitate the prostheticization of the Indian, on the one hand, and consolidation of whiteness as property, on the other.

Through a queer of color lens, we can see that such a "primitive"—even tribal—family unit introduces the heteronormative gender relations of the American family as the mechanism through which gendered divisions of labor secure pioneer masculinity. Turnerian frontier logics make heteronormative labor more central, thereby making the "slavery question" subsidiary to the frontier thesis, and thus mystifying Black bodies' contributions to the political ecology of colonial frontier life. Queer of color theory allows us to reassess the frontier thesis as the entrenchment of colonial forms of heteronormativity and racism that critique must undo. In *Aberrations in Black: Towards a Queer of Color Critique*, sociologist Roderick Ferguson problematizes the ways that leftist theories arguing for economic liberation collude with bourgeois heteronormativity. Marxist analysis might critique the class-based values of ruling elite capitalists in economic terms but leave undertheorized the ways that racial, gendered, and sexual normativity shape the bourgeois values that they supposedly decry. Queer of color critique understands and centers this unexpected collusion of leftist and capitalist ideology in their mutual denigration of the sexually perverse.

The home, with the nationalist ideologies that underpin it, mechanizes an instrument of nationalist exclusion. The figuration of a domestic sphere of bourgeois heteronuclearity renders subjects that are incommensurate with or, perhaps, un-houseable within the homestead. I mark a colonial imaginary in the Turnerian frontier that underwrites the property logics of domestic exclusion of queers and queers of color. This is a fundamental critique of liberal capitalism that is formative of queer of color critique more generally. Ferguson, citing Chandan Reddy, decries "the silences that both Marxism and liberal pluralism share" in their surreptitiously cooperative "expulsion of queers of color from literal homes [and] from the privileges bestowed by the nation as 'home.'"[60] Directly quoting Reddy, Ferguson puts forward:

> Unaccounted for within both Marxist and liberal pluralist discussions of the home and the nation, queers of color as people of color . . . take up the critical task of both remembering and rejecting the model of the 'home' offered in the United States in two ways: first, by attending to the ways in which it was defined over and against people of color, and second, by expanding the locations and moments of that critique of the home to interrogate processes of group formation and self-formation from the experience of being expelled from their own dwellings and families for not conforming to the dictation of and demand for uniform gendered and sexual types.[61]

Naturally, the "demand for uniform gendered and sexual types" revolves around normative constructions of the family. The theme of home and the queer "homeless," so to speak, is an essential element that carries through to Ferguson's intervention of a "queer of color critique," reading "racial formations, as they are constituted nonnormatively by gender and sexual differences, [which] overdetermine national identity, contradicting its manifold promises of citizenship and property."[62] This comes to a head in queer of color's immanent critique of leftist ideology, particularly in Ferguson's meticulous reading of *The German Ideology*, in which Marx problematically reifies colonial racist ideologies as constitutively part of his revolutionary disidentification with capitalism. Ferguson tracks the ways "Marx universalized heteropatriarchy as he theorized property ownership . . . within the tribe"[63] by citing the following compelling passage:

> The first form of ownership is tribal . . . ownership . . . The division of labor is at [this] stage still very elementary and is confined to a further extension of the *natural* division of labour existing in the family. The social structure is, therefore, limited to an extension of the family; patriarchal family chieftains, below them the members of the tribe, finally slaves.[64]

Indeed, Ferguson discovers that Marx himself relied on colonial anthropological definitions of the "primitive family" in order to naturalize patriarchal divisions of labor as tribally and therefore *naturally* derived organizations of human work along gendered and heteronormative lines. The male is at the head of the household, while women assume the duties of the domestic space. Patriarchy ineluctably shapes Marxian understandings of legitimate ways to cultivate human labor capacities. However, since colonial racism undergirds political understandings of the exploitation of such capacities, the conscientization of a proletarian class as the only morally just historical movement toward a reorganization of society carries with it some risks. These include the reification of an unspoken coloniality structuring Western capitalist societies *and* proposed communist alternatives to such societies. Put more simply, the proletarian class derives its class consciousness in contradistinction to the bourgeois class partly by disavowing capitalism's role in colonialism. Turner and Marx, then, are not that distinct in their reproduction of a heteronormative racial state, whether in Europe or on the frontier. It matters little whether the dialectic traversing the state is that of the capitalist versus the proletarian or that of the colonial pioneer and his property. Both dyads would be systems in which neither the Indian nor the slave owns their own labor—labor which can be cultivated free from exploitation. Or, as Marx poetically put it: this is uncompromised labor in which the "Realm of Freedom" is divested from the "Realm of Necessity."[65]

The pioneer family and the pioneer head of its household obtain their prominence in the political economy of the frontier, in its relation to the de-coupling of slavery from American history. Heteronormativity as a frontier-construct is what underwrites different racial parameters for understanding US expansion. Put another way, colonial heteronormativity is one of the main mechanisms through which the frontier prosthesis actualizes its consumption of native culture, and thus habilitates a white able body to transform frontier into property. The white homestead—constructed, cultivated, and coordinated by the pioneer—is an institution of the US racial state. Because this homestead is shaped through clear gendered divisions of labor and around the heteronuclear family, sexual politics are an inherent aspect of the Turnerian frontier. The frontier prosthesis in which both land and ability become propertied aspects of the American subject, on the one hand, and the appropriation of the indigenous body, on the other, also is an instantiation of what theorist Scott Lauria Morgensen calls "settler sexuality." He defines this as "a white national heteronormativity that regulates Indigenous sexuality and gender by supplanting them with the sexual modernity of settler subjects."[66] While Turner does not explicitly write about indigenous sexuality, the prostheticization of the native body as a scaffold for the white able-body facilitates the capacity of the pioneer to comply with and enact the heteronormative colonialism central to the implantation of the homestead. So, the relative primitivism of the Indian is, indeed, supplanted "with the sexual modernity of settler subjects" whose own civilization is never really threatened by the savagery of the frontier because of the presence of white heteronormative relations. Savagery is kept at bay because the land is made straight. In a compelling way, this is part of the answer to theorist Mark Rifkin's question of "when did Indians became straight?"[67] A partial answer is: when ability manifested as a form of white property *and* when this property became the colonial site for the heteronormative American family. The Indian becomes straight insofar as such an identity is coupled with and augments the ability of the pioneer able-body whose capacities sustain and reproduce colonial logics of heteronormativity. Because the Indian is a prosthetic device articulated to the settler body, and this settler body is coded as straight, in a rather direct way, the exploration of the presumed heterosexuality of the Indian is inseparable from a disability analysis. Dis/ability is an indissoluble part of the ways that both sexual and racial logics shape regimes of the colonial.

## Conclusion: A US Empire Studies of Disability

In this chapter, I have attempted to show that the imperial bodymind that emerges from the crucible of manifest domesticity and Manifest Destiny is one fertile critical genealogy of US empire studies captured by manifest disablement. That is, I have attempted to show that US empire studies—and American studies more broadly—should pay critical heed to the ways that logics of ableism and colonialism mutually inform and constitute each other. While the idea is not developed within the space of this chapter, I wish to emphasize that I have come to this analysis as a Filipinx American critic. It is from this positionality that I make concluding remarks about future critical orientations that take seriously the colonial and racial life of disability. A more critical Asian American studies most certainly should understand how the time in which the "Pacific" entered American imperial vocabulary coincided with Turner's authorship. He wrote during a time of great crisis in American masculinity. This crisis provoked a turn toward the Pacific, wherein "the meeting point between civilization and savagery" would play out with other "indios" and Indians to be similarly consumed, appropriated, and dispossessed.[68] Might US Empire be a systematic imposition of racialized disablement around whose organizing locus is a white masculine able-body?

Because the "boundedness" of home is inextricably tied to the "boundlessness" of empire, the domestic figuration of the heteronormative homestead as a feature of white property depends on the propertied dispossession of Indigenous, Black, and (later) Asian subjects.[69] The linkages between manifest domesticity and the imperial drive of Manifest Destiny intersect in the figuration of racialized subjects that cannot inhabit Euramerican Enlightenment rationality; such subjects thus cannot be "a subject without properties" endowed with deeds to property.[70] American civilized whiteness and the primitivity of the frontier can exist in logical non-contradiction because racialized white able-bodiedness is coupled with the able-mindedness of the enlightenment subject whose sovereignty is unquestioned. As my crip analysis has shown, the autology of the white pioneer body exists as a self-determining agent because of its appropriation of a native body—a process that I have captured as a form of "frontier prosthesis."

The "manliness" of civilization, as it has been characterized by historian Gail Bederman, sees an epistemological flashpoint in the frontier historicism of Turner.[71] Manliness required rehabilitation—an infusion of vitality whose proving ground would be the epistemological invention of the frontier. As Turnerian theory cultivated a safe space for masculinity, it did so by binding the frontier with the contractual obligations of property whose stewardship required a sound mind and robust body to ensure the transformation of the wilds into a truly American civilization. Turner authored this particular American social contract to circumvent an epochal crisis for masculinity at the very moment the "frontier line" had been removed from the 1890 census, "mark[ing] the closing of a great historic movement"—the frontier had ended.[72] It should not surprise the reader that the late nineteenth was a century of tremendous racial and transnational transition for the United States, whose imperial century of transpacific expansion was about to begin in earnest. The Philippines and other territories became objects of US conquest partially as a result of the ableist invention of and need to extend the frontier. This crisis in masculinity, as it has been examined by various feminist historians, resulted in a reinvigorated martial masculinity contradistinguished from the effeminate masculinities of "little brown brothers."[73] The debilitations of the frontier, the prosthesis of indigeneity as a suture to American white masculinity, the crystallization of American civilization through the prophylactic of white frontier heteronormativity, and the contractual capacities central to the moral justifications of imperialism all set the discursive stage for the rehabilitative powers of empire.

Manifest disablement describes how the frontier thesis projected the frontier as a westward march of civilization whose movement dispossessed through racialization and thereby accreted ability as a function of property ownership. Reading the intersection of disability and imperialism reorients not only the frontier's relationship to American embodiment, but also nuances the spatial expanse of the frontier as an interminable horizon of opportunity. The frontier is a kind of futurity for a body that is corporeally and spiritually whole. This is in contradistinction to the kinds of temporalities theorized by crip theorists. So-called "crip temporalities" speak of disabled existence not as a form of living that is mortgaged on their deviation from the wholeness of the able-body (which, naturally, is assumed to have the best prospects and greatest chance of happiness).[74] Instead, crip theory envisions futures that do not malign interdependence, and that look with suspicion upon uncritical endorsements of self-determination—definitions of which have clear, if often obscured, colonial antecedents. Such liberal independence is defined by a form of individualism in which the human is radically independent and self-reliant. However, this liberal human's individual sovereignty is defined tacitly in relation to a capitalist society to which they can contribute productively. What might we gain in a critical ethnic studies project that orients its imagination of a futurity of social justice toward the kinds of crip temporalities that similarly imagine alternatives to neoliberal individualism? Might the ethical question for the contemporary moment be to theorize more judiciously *whom* we center, even provisionally so, as the subject of social protest, to be sure that the project of critique does not reify historical, sedimented logics of ableism? When marginal voices vie to reclaim agency, upon which logics precisely is such agentive subjectivity articulated?

As I have established in this historical-discursive treatment of the myth of Manifest Destiny, the Americanization of the frontier body confronts the threshold of its own fragile capacities. Europe's debilities are set aside to prioritize, instead, a settler reconstruction of the American body to navigate the harsh realities of western colonial expansion. Turner's "frontier thesis" is really a "frontier prosthesis," commodifying Indian ability for its adroit and hale capacities to achieve what European cosmopolitanism never could: the furtherance of the white race and the heteronormative state in inhospitable terrain. The horizon of the frontier became a psychic drive tantalizing the American bodymind.

This chapter has thus established that US racial capitalism predisposes us to the seductions of racial interchangeability—an engine of so-called American innovation, heteronuclear reproductive politics, and a racial fetishism for the other to augment the deficiencies of the citizen; this system thus supports the persistent fantasy of individualistic freedom and independence that constrain our ethical imagination while lining our pockets. *Dos X* will now pivot from the historic American West to the Latinx-Filipinx Borderlands. While the ethical drama of white American fetishization and subsequent prosthetization of the Indian body present a clearly vertical relationship authored by racial-colonial power, I move away from the *bildung* of the pioneer and to a contemporary coming-of-age narrative embroiled in horizontal modes of racial interchange. The ethical guideposts we desire in the face of colonial violence are not as available in the modern Chicano-Filipino tale offered to us by Filipinx-American author Brian Ascalon Roley that I take up in the next chapter.

# 2 | Filipinx Spanish

## *Crip Genres of Anti-Assimilation*

"Don't you overstand me with your flip, peasant Spanish!"

Tomas, *American Son*

In this chapter, I examine a perplexing yet not entirely unexpected encounter of Filipinx and Chicanx masculinity in the Los Angeles Borderlands in Carlos Bulosan's short story "The Romance of Magno Rubio" and Brian Ascalon Roley's novel *American Son*. I explore Roley's novel in conjunction with other literary and cultural works that constellate the cross-racial encounters I wish to analyze. An aspect of the terrain upon which I scrutinize the *choque* of Filipino and Chicano racial embodiment is the inability to speak Spanish—a state of incapacity that perennially marks Filipino postcoloniality yet constitutes Philippine national histories of cognitive sovereignty; Spanish was and continues to be the language of enlightenment in Philippine historical constructions of nationalist development. Philippine Spanish can be an object of nostalgia, or it can constitute a melancholic relation to a past of haute culture that materializes unevenly in the present.[1] I measure inability to speak Spanish in a structural and cultural sense, rather than in an individual's capacity to acquire the language. The reality is that the Philippines is not a Hispanophone country, thus rendering Spanish as a lost object that was never truly present in the first place. I do not mean to suggest that the Spanish language and Hispanic culture are minimal presences in Philippine culture; this would be far from accurate. Rather, the result of Spanish colonialism in the Philippines was not the linguistic erasure of Indigenous languages—a reality that requires a more nuanced understanding and exploration of the linguistic politics of (in the instance of this chapter) the diaspora of the Philippines. Alongside creole languages like Chavacano, Philippine, or Filipinx, Spanish is, I suggest, a phantom linguistic repertoire of speech and action, reflecting more the realities of absence, distance, and dismemberment than an enduring and wide-ranging empirical presence. I ponder expanding the parameters through which we understand creolization and creolized subjectivities by thinking of the ways that cultural echoes of Filipinx Spanish are represented in the US-Mexico Borderlands. I distinguish "Filipinx Spanish" from "Philippine Spanish" for the purpose of this study, differentiating Asian American diasporic constructions of Hispanic culture from those of the Philippines.

By focusing on diasporic renditions of this repertoire of fantasmatic speech, it becomes clear that the history of elite Hispano-Philippine intellectual culture stands in contradistinction to the ways that Spanish is understood in the United States as pertaining to an underclass of laborers. I wish to denaturalize that elitist relation in order to expand the itineraries through which we can capture the archives of Filipinx Spanish. I use "Filipinx Spanish" intentionally to reflect on the rapprochement of this linguistic repertoire with Latinx linguistic formations, and to distinguish it from archives of Philippine Spanish more often associated with the distant historical past. The co-formation of Filipinx and Chicano Spanishes is the crossroads I prioritize to examine the intersections of disability in racial capitalism. My suggestion is that literature and literary genres of assimilation offer a window to understand the ways that ability and political economy intersect. The goal of assimilation is to engineer immigrants into the hale robust laborers that US racial capitalism requires. I hope to disturb that aesthetic principle. The Philippine cultural archives that are constellated through Spanish are a topic that I have written about in previous work, which I bring forward to examine the formation of diasporic Filipinx experience. Yet, arguing that diasporic Filipinx Spanish and canonical Philippine Spanish produced by the *ilustrados* at the turn of the twentieth century represent entirely different genealogical configurations does a disservice to both their multifarious origins. Partly rooting one's perspective in an Asian rendition of mestizaje, it is intriguing to note that authors of the Philippine nationalist movements were themselves the material and intellectual product of mixed origins and traditions—Spanish, Filipino, Mexican, Chinese, and, later, Filipino American. The ethnolinguistic diversity of the Philippines notwithstanding, Philippine Hispanic culture has always been the product of overlapping contact zones, and could be said to be a Borderlands configuration in itself. Engaging with Filipino-Chicano intersections simultaneously challenges the dominant colonial ideals of Philippine Spanish identity, such as it is, while also being an organic outgrowth of the multivalent and hybrid ways in which

Filipinx identity has always navigated complex multiple intersecting identities. This chapter thus focuses on the curious case of Filipinx racial drag as Mexican. "Filipinx" in this case best modifies "racial drag," as it captures the unstable nature of Filipinx identity that has been elaborated at various points in *Dos X*. Additionally, the term captures the ways in which racial ambivalence maps onto and is productive of gender non-conformity. It is the intersections of racial mutability and gender non-conformity that I explore. Racialized Mexican drag is a performative whose construction is enabled by the multiplicative inventories of brownness, braided labor histories, and cultural proximities that are germane to the state of California in the United States. While a Filipinx version of *Mexicanidad* might appear jarring, given the intersectional ethnic and racial landscape I cover, such horizontal racial appropriations could arguably be inevitable, rather than exceptional.

Filipinx Mexican drag constitutes a labyrinthine racial border crossing, improbably conceived by Mexican and Philippine nationalist intellectuals like Octavio Paz, José Vasconcelos, Pedro Paterno, and José Rizal.[2] And yet their theorizations of racial formation, problematic in many instances, demonstrate the ways that racial ambivalence is the rule rather than the exception. I invite an intersecting comparative study of US Latinx and Filipinx culture through the absent presence of Spanish—thinking through a disability analysis of linguistic capacities that turn on the absent presences of Philippine Spanish in the US-Mexican Borderlands. "Filipinx Spanish" in the US Mexico Borderlands is an unexpected yet, I argue, vital cultural archive that speaks to the possibility of painful misrecognitions. It also indexes heuristic parameters through which we can assess the deeply sedimented colonial histories that inform diasporic comparative racialization.[3] These connections, I contend, are mapped best through a crip analysis.

As I have been articulating across the case studies of *Dos X*, the relationship between the sovereign institution of the American citizen and the alien migrant labor is foundationally authored as an ableist extractive relation to migrant labor power. In short, the ostensive liberal independence of the citizen has relied historically on the physical labor capacities of the alien laborer to subsidize the myth of able-bodied independence. Filipinx and Mexican American intersections are one important cultural case study to understand the ways that comparative and relational racialization crucially constructs this ableist labor relation. Able-bodied constructions of the ethnic migrant laborer pinpoint idealized physical capacities that inexorably filter and occasion racial-labor substitutability as coextensive with subordination. Therefore, racialized impressions of what we could call "Filipinx" and "Mexican American" or "Latino" personhood are prostheticized and grafted onto this ontological laboring body fetishized by American racial capitalism.

Mexican Americans and Filipinx Americans are both in the US West and Southwest partly because of the shared colonial encounters each historically has with Spain and the United States. I hope to offer a literary and cultural reading that models a robust comparative race analysis. In doing so, I suggest that we scope "Filipinx Spanish" within and as a comparative racial lens that enhances racial and colonial studies within disability and crip critique. The ways that this manifests, I argue, are through the thematic and racial aesthetic representation of American assimilation. This genre of migrant literature can align with the normalizing regimes of assimilation in order to produce competent able-bodied laborers that comply with the mandates of ableist racial capitalism. This literature can also aid us in imaginatively constructing alternatives or dissent.

I suggest that migrant diaspora anti-assimilation becomes a critical language of disability. It transforms into a vector of critique of the very institutions and discourses that shape ideal alien laborers and the myth of unfettered social mobility, as a worker whose labors ought to contribute advantage to US society. Such a healthful society would be harmed by the inclusion of disabled people who cannot comply with the work required to make society hale and functional under liberal independent models of political economy. The alien is invited, indeed, required to comply with this structure of racial capitalist ableism; their body is made to conform to exploitative ideals of physical capacity creating the racialized substrate upon which the able-bodied citizen rests their head. Immigration is historically structured as an evaluative enterprise determining the level of contribution the immigrant body can furnish for and as capital. These determinations have been balanced by the ableist paranoia in which deficient migrants would potentially become wards of the state.[4] My question is whether misrecognition within the very racial landscape in which bodies are identified as prime capital for extraction disrupts the discursive mechanisms through which such exploitation materializes. In this sense, ableism becomes a tacit structure of migrant inclusion, given that the prevailing economic system has historically required racialized alien labor to reproduce itself. For this reason, assimilation in multiethnic literature is an important cultural and literary archive in examining how these logics materialize and how they can be critiqued.

Migrant literature broaches the theme of assimilation or adaptation into new cultural milieus—the migrant body is the site of adaptation, exploitation, and literary innovation. As queer diasporas theory has evidenced, literary and cultural genres explore the profound ways that the diasporic subjectivity of the migrant is braided with a cultural or national environment that is typically inhospitable or hostile to racial and sexual difference. The incentive to normalize is palpable. Furthermore, cultural normalization indexed in migrant literature evinces the desire for normative labor to reproduce the socio-economic systems in which assimilation is articulated as an unproblematic good. Nevertheless, Gayatri Gopinath, Martin Manalansan, and David Eng have shown the ways that a resistant subject formation of the sexual-minority migrant produces antinormative or alternative frameworks from which to examine both the nation-state of arrival and the national homelands from whence migrants hailed. In his article "Migrating Like a Queen," cultural theorist Ruben Zecena has similarly explored the ways that queer, trans, and gender-nonconforming migrants coalesce their struggles in a collective transmigrant community, simultaneously complying with US asylum law while reading against the grain of the US cis-heteropartriarchy that structures the terms of national belonging.[5] Although one could argue that assimilation is a professed goal of these gender non-conforming transmigrants, this is done by interrogating the conditions of inclusion of that assimilation. Indeed, Zecena's work offers a compelling opportunity to read with resistant migrant subjects that question the terms of national inclusion on the basis of hegemonic norms. Instead, transmigrants point to political grammars of anti-assimilation. Such an archive also points to the ways that racial and gender non-conforming migrant cultures are a vital discourse in unraveling the ableist assumptions that structure the institution of citizenship. The stakes are not only who can be a citizen but also the opening up of the archives of embodiment to unsettle the racial-ableist assumptions that structure ideologies of citizenship in the first place.

I thus attempt to locate and analyze an aesthetic structure of anti-assimilation whose logical and political orientation is rooted in transmigrant identity. I mark the "trans" of transmigrant as an itinerant subjectivity that forms part of what Victor Román Mendoza has called a "queer nomadology."[6] I configure this nomadic orientation as a Filipinx response to Octavio Paz's labyrinthine, caustic, and anxious defense of Mexican masculinity from the dangers and anxiety of penetration. Extending and interrogating Paz's metaphysical (and, in some cases, literal) ideations of penetration, the racial misrecognition of the brown bodies of Mexicans and Filipinx Americans represent one kind of interpenetration I seek to explore.[7] The ways in which I explore peripatetic renditions of Mexican masculinity are actually through Filipinx inhabitations of it. As with other parts of this book, I am concerned here with transracial forms of drag that amalgamate subject formations and inventories of identity that 1. question the empirical structure through which we fetishize the stability of racial-national identity claims as constituting a fact about us, and 2. locate a form of agency constructed through a transracial solidarity rooted ironically in misrecognition (for another). My point here (as well as in this entire monograph) is to author modes of collective being that respect difference, while also inhabiting the logics of racial capitalism that occasion one's misrecognition for another as a matter of racist misapprehension. As I have been arguing, the very fact of these misrecognitions indexes a structural feature of racial capitalism that, on the one hand, demands uniform and mutually substitutable units of labor, and, on the other, indexes the ways that racial formations are *co-formal* constructions whose foundation is shared coloniality. In uncovering such co-formations, I urge a mode of multimigrant and transracial alterity—to invoke Emmanuel Levinas—that conjures an ethical orientation toward another, grounded partly in racial-capitalist interchangeability that questions the ways that such interchangeability nourishes the logics of assimilation. Filipinx racial drag as a Mexican is the aesthetic case study I think through in this chapter; rather than prioritizing a critique of appropriation, I suspend that critique in favor of (for now) the ways that this racial error produces different kinds of shared realities and kinships in which assimilation is not solely measured through the measuring stick of embodying whiteness.

I understand that the use of terms like "drag" and the prefix "trans" inevitably allude to transgender or transsexual identities. This is a live connection, as trans studies has certainly greatly impacted the ways in which I think about cross-racial encounter, identification, and transformation. For instance, Cameron Awkward-Rich, Cassius Adair, Kadji Amin, and Susan Stryker have each explored various epistemologies of gender non-conformity and their relations with sexuality, colonialism, and disability studies.[8] What these authors help to demonstrate is that transgender identity formations are also racial formations. Or, rather, these show the ways in which both understandings of gender and how it is transed often are imbricated in systems of racial classification. As I observe throughout this book, racial misrecognition and racial drag often are a tactical response to the dispossessions that occur due to racialized effeminacy. For this reason, I am compelled by the ways that C. Riley Snorton has elaborated upon formations of, not simply race or gender, but rather "racialized gender."[9] In this chapter, I track the ways that Mexican American and Filipinx American racial formation may inhabit the same body despite having a specious claim to such identities. What I mean by this is that Filipinx American embodiment in Borderlands spaces along Mexico is marked by Mexican American racial formation as much as it is marked by Asian American racialization. I am interested in examining the ways in which these racial projects interlock in the production and molding of Filipinx subjectivity as a literary and aesthetic project. Even when one's subjective response to misrecognition is to correct, such misattributions are still evidence of the braided nature of racial subjectivity and identity. My purpose is not to evaluate the facticity of identitarian claims, but rather to observe the ways in which socio-political circumstances that would give impetus to such multifarious claims are grounded in a disavowed intersectional history of colonial encounter. What we might call "the racial error of misrecognition" is actually a heuristic that allows an examination of the multivalent discourses and histories that produce the conditions of possibility for both migrant encounter and the fear of racial interchangeability in the first place. Such encounters, I suggest, are bound up with trajectories and developmentalist teloses of assimilation whose narrative permutations are likewise ineluctably tied up with ability. In the following section, I want to describe what I mean in calling assimilation and its resistances a "crip genre." In order to define this term, it becomes necessary to articulate how aesthetic and narrative conventions fit within a system of racial capitalism.

## Crip Genre of Anti-Assimilation

Filipinx migrant literature, I suggest, aids us in mapping the trajectories of the cross-racial encounters constitutive of what I am putting forth as the crip genre of anti-assimilation. Filipinx Spanish becomes a marker of linguistic relation, indexing subterranean colonial encounters between Spanish and US colonialism that have spurned the braided migrant subjectivities of Mexican and Filipinx Americans. An argument of this book is that the franchise of US citizenship is constructed through ableist and disabling capitalist extraction. Racialized alien labor historically has been configured as the disabled underside propping up US fictions of independence. Sovereign, capacitated citizenship compels an understanding of labor to be atomistic and individually propertied, rather than a construction where the rigid borders of the nation required non-citizen bodies and their capacities to produce the illusion of unfettered individualism. That is to say, ability itself is a racialized property of the American citizen—ability *is* property. While I explored this vis-à-vis historical renditions of the US frontier in the first chapter, here I seek to understand how literary economies of assimilation reflect or dissent from the myth of the liberal individual as able-bodied agent within the Borderlands spaces that were subjected to historical colonial configurations of the frontier. The liberal individual's ability mortgages and subsidizes its existence through its disavowed historical and material relation to migrant alien labor.

Given this theoretical context, I gesture toward a crip genre of anti-assimilation to challenge the frontier nostalgia through which ableist assimilations and appropriations were mapped into the very idea of America. In the vein of literary and cultural representations of capacity, what I capture as an aesthetic of anti-assimilation questions the migrant conventions that would demand normalization, and even integration, into respectable capitalist economies. Additionally, this aesthetic subjects to scrutiny both whiteness and the model minority as the capacitated goals or telos of Asian Americanization. It foregrounds other kinds of affinity and kinship in permutations that are horizontal—rather than those that are vertical (and thus uncritically and upwardly mobile). Indeed, this kind of horizontality is part of the motivation of theorizing from a perspective of dos x.

The present chapter attempts to explore this argument in the context of literary representations of assimilation. Typically, the topic of assimilation in multiethnic American literature explores ethnic protagonists that assimilate upwardly into whiteness or, perhaps, offers representational opportunities to disidentify with the project of assimilation. I am interested in this aspect of racial drag; however, rather than vertical assimilation, I consider cross-racial horizontal assimilation. Indeed, given the right framing, we can call assimilation into respectable whiteness a form of racial drag that is the precondition of full material citizenship. Citizenship is the product of racial drag—we saw this in a way with Frederick Jackson Turner in the previous chapter. In the current chapter, in contrast, I seek to understand the collision of the ethnic masculinity of the Mexican gangster and the hyper-femininity of the effeminate Asian American archetypes in the Filipino anti-assimilation narrative present in Roley's *American Son*. Filipinx America in the Mexican Borderlands shifts the meanings of Spanish from the enlightened able-minded subject of the Philippine archipelago to the debilitated linguistic capacities of the amalgamated Filipinx-Chicanx subject, marked by deviant criminality, pathological motherhood, and the racial-sexual pathologies of Asian effeminacy—all scoped within the debilitating crosshairs of multiple colonialisms.

In order to disentangle the ableist assumptions upon which normative assimilation narrative in minority fiction operates, the present chapter employs a dialogical, comparative framework, incorporating Chicana theories of the border-as-bodily-impairment, or "herida abierta" (open wound), and adding these to Filipino psycholinguistic debilities that I associate with Philippine Hispanicity. Such a dialogue renders the project of coherent sovereignty through robust language-making a dubious proposition. I stage this dialogue in order to understand the ways in which Filipinx masculinities interact with Chicanx masculinity in the US-Mexican borderscape, assuming the pathological criminality of the Cholo/Mexican subject and the racially castrated debilitated embodiment of the Filipinx/Asian American subject. I suggest that this racial spectrum of gender and sexuality (the ethnic masculinity of the Mexican gangster at one end, the colonial femininity of the Asian body at the other) invites engagement with theoretical formations that have dealt with racialized articulations of gender and sexuality. Specifically, this dialogue brings into conversation queer Asian American studies critiques of Orientalist effeminacy with feminist border theory around linguistic sovereignty—the preservation of defective Spanish over and against Anglophone normalization and Castilian respectability. I situate this comparative ethnic studies framework within disability theory. I argue that it is through a feminist and queer of color disability framework that we can understand the comparative affinities of Filipinx and Latinx subject formations along the herida abierta wherein identity is already seemingly in flux and contingent. *American Son* focuses on two overlapping, yet distinct, phenomena: a disability genre I am calling the anti-assimilation narrative, and the historical inability of Filipinos to speak Spanish what Roley calls "flip, peasant Spanish."

Roley crips the genre of assimilation narrative through comparative racialization. Instead of the Asian American male subject assimilating into a "respectable" subject position consonant with the prevailing trope of the "model minority"—endowed with a seemingly endless cognitive ability surpassing and thriving because of white supremacy—the Filipinx American brothers Tomas and Gabe embrace and strategically embody the seemingly pathological criminal attachments of Chicano masculinity. As a narrative device, this cross-racial drag can stage a much-needed critique of assimilation narratives that advance racial fetish, respectability, and the articulation of an Asian American subject that is anti-Black and anti-Latino.[10] What can a non-deficit-based reading of pathology bring to Asian American studies, and can it unravel the model minority myth? The presentation of, on the one hand, Roley's character Tomas as a figure that rescripts Asian American masculinity and, on the other, his brother Gabe as a figure whose *bildung* is the assimilation into Latinidad can, I suggest, reorient—indeed, crip—assimilation narratives that demand a character coming into proper coherent subjectivity. However, such moves can and do problematically reinscribe the racist pathologies of criminality. The American sons' cross-racial drag also re-substantiates the problematic co-constitution of Asian effeminacy and Latino criminality as modes of defective or toxic masculinity needing rehabilitative intervention. In this reading, the misrecognition of Filipinos as Latinos in the Borderlands becomes less about comparative racial affinity or coalitional politics, and more about a US racial imaginary grounded in white supremacy. This problem precipitates my crip, queer turn to the failures of Asian assimilation and the model minority that it stubbornly inaugurates as the desirable, respectable subject of Asian America. I turn, then, to the "wounded tongues" of Chicana feminism by way of defective "peasant, Flip Spanish."

I highlight the deficit of Spanish through a disability lens in order to enable a comparative ethnic studies method. This theme of wounded Spanishes will surface again in future chapters. I frame the ways in which normalizing modes of minority assimilation narration productively fail through the absent presence of Spanish in Filipino American literature. Perhaps ironically, it is through the linguistic absence of Spanish (or, more deliberately, because of particularized colonial histories of Spain in the Philippines—the linguistic incapacity of the Filipino to speak Spanish despite being a former denizen of the Spanish Empire) constituting the Filipino American "tongue" (to borrow from Gloria Anzaldúa) that a conversation can be staged between the Borderlands of the US-Philippines and the US-Mexico.[11] Put another way, by drawing on disability frameworks that problematize the "positive" capacities to perform as a fully formed and coherent subject, we can question longstanding albeit implicit notions of Hispanophone inability as a lack that needs to be fixed in order to bring the Philippines into the Hispanic culture. Perhaps, ironically, Filipinx American studies has approached this question neurodivergently, through a canonical figure: the migrant illiterate. While Brian Ascalon Roley's novel forms a bulwark of the analysis of this chapter, in the next section, I begin with an analysis of Carlos Bulosan's short story "The Romance of Magno Rubio" as a historical precursor to the

Latinx-Filipinx literary aesthetic that is elaborated in Roley's *American Son*. I think that we can make a case to include Bulosan's short story as an earlier iteration—and thus foundational part—of a comparative migrant archive that tracks the co-formal relationships I attempt to track throughout *Dos X*. While the term "flip peasant" is invoked by Roley to demonstrate the derogated subject position of Filipinx migrants in the late-twentieth-century United States, the racial and politico-economic dimensions of the term describe the realities of Filipinx laborers in the early twentieth century, as represented by Bulosan.

## Diasporic Impairments: On the Disability of Filipinx Migration

I begin with a canonical text that has attenuated Filipinx American studies understandings of the comparative construction of Filipinx masculinity in the US-Mexican Borderlands. What I hope to get at in this section is the way in which migrant literature elaborates American racial formation, racialized labor, and—following a feminist disability analytic—the cognitive ability that attaches to Asian American subject formations. However, for Filipinx America, as with other Asian groups, the end result of assimilation into American subjectivity is *not* the enlightened model minority. Contemporary Filipinx American cultural representations of the work of Carlos Bulosan continue to inform understandings of race, gender, and sexuality as a productive comparative border aesthetic, and to contribute to understanding the Borderlands as a cognitive landscape. I am thinking here of Lonnie Carter's theatrical adaptations that foreground Bulosan's story as a Borderlands narrative. Reading the Borderlands as a cognitive landscape takes up Gloria Anzaldúa's reading of the border as herida abierta via a Filipino American studies analytic of itinerant labor. I advance this reading through Carlos Bulosan's flip peasant and illiterate anti-capitalist stoop laborer Magno Rubio.

Lonnie Carter's 2003 play "The Romance of Magno Rubio," based on the Bulosan short story of the same name, narrates the stoop labor of a bachelor quintet of Filipinos working as migrant seasonal laborers in the fields of California's central valley in the 1930s. Like the play it inspires, the original story narrates the epistolary love affair that its titular character, Magno Rubio, has with the American Dream, embodied by the hulking feminine whiteness of Clarabelle. Significantly, language is not a transparent medium through which Rubio can express love and devotion; his illiteracy is configured as an incapacity that precludes direct communication. Rubio spends his meager wages courting Clarabelle, who ultimately deceives him, illustrating lucidly the treachery that America's capitalist expansion holds for its cheap labor inputs. Bulosan, as we will see below, foregrounds a jarring juxtaposition of the illiteracy of Magno Rubio and the epistolary mechanism through which he woos Clarabelle. Carter's theatrical reproduction and reimagining of this foundational short story in Filipino American literature reconfigures Bulosan's literary/epistolary incapacity through, perhaps ironically, the multilinguality of Filipino racialization. One series of lines in Carter's play demonstrates the multiracial and comparative aspects of this Filipino American cultural text:

> Magno Rubio Filipino boy / Magno Rubio Filipi—Pinoy . . . /
> Now picking peas in the San Jose hills / A quarter an hour don't pay our bills/
> In rain, shine, or mudslide, he's always stooped/
> *Pagod na pagod, palaging* pooped/
> He's not without hope, *todos los días*/
> *Fantasía amor* for all the señoritas/
> One sticks in his brain and drains his *cabeza*/
> With jugs of wine and *fría cerveza*.[12]

How do we translate the Spanish alongside the Tagalog in these lines? Does it reference an erstwhile Hispanization of the Philippines under the Spanish Crown? Does it attempt to conjure the Hispanic identity of the Filipino? Or does it simply demonstrate an attentiveness to the space of the US-Mexican border in narratives of US Filipino migration? How might we understand such an invocation of Philippine Hispanicity within the US-Mexican Borderlands? I suggest that we understand the polysemous appearance of multilingualism alongside the illiteracy of Bulosan's "big blonde" through a disability reading.

But why disability? Apart from the understanding of the contradictions between meritocratic democracy and capitalism as itself a racialized mind-body split, the kinds of bodily and cognitive divergences tracked by disability studies are series of phenomena assiduously chronicled in ethnic studies and, as such, can be understood within the critical operations of feminist disability. To be clear, such a reorientation of these fields of inquiry does not suggest one should bring disability studies to ethnic studies in order to revise its foundational claims; rather, it is to demonstrate how ethnic studies theories have always been mobilizing critical operations central to disability studies. Chicana and Filipina feminist works are the examples of woman of color feminist disability that I elaborate in the space of this essay. Although Asian American histories have sought to challenge the accumulation of racial capital through dispossession by highlighting the contradiction between egalitarian liberal democracy and the need for cheap racialized labor, the capacities necessary to perform the bodily labors required of capitalist accumulation are persistently interrogated within the perceived deficient mental capacities of the perverse Asian immigrant. Put more bluntly, yet abstractly, the international division of labor required to sustain the aporia between liberal democracy and labor exploitation is also an international division of cognitive capacity. In this way, Lisa Lowe's foundational critique of the systematic contradiction from which American capitalist democracy derives sustenance articulates a mind-body split within the institution of American citizenship.[13] I find this suggestion convincing if we understand American citizenship (indeed, part of the American Dream discourse consonant with respectable Asian immigrant acts) to be the foundation of robust political life. The capacities required to participate as fully realized, whole, civil subjects endowed and secured within American constitutional democracy have an underside. As argued in Asian American studies, this underside is the de-minded, expendable, and substitutable racialized bodies who represent the labor inputs necessary to ensure the possibility and imaginability of robust political life.[14] The aesthetics in Anzaldúa's poetic configuration of the border as an herida abierta are foundational to how women of color theoretical constructions of subjectivity have been attentive to bodily impairment as well as the neurodivergent subjectivities that are mediated by multiple languages.[15] We shall thus see that the multiple racial affinities of Filipino American identity, produced through the historical intersections of both American manifest transpacific expansion and Spanish imperialism, are marked by linguistic deficit: the inarticulacy and incapacity of the Filipino to speak Spanish—the wounded tongues of what Roley calls Flip Spanish. In this way, I suggest that this fractured version of Hispanic modernity, as it is articulated through the inarticulacy of the Filipino tongue, is an important comparative ethnic studies intervention.[16]

The multilinguality of Rubio's migrant existence is not remarkable simply because his subjectivity apparently needs three languages to be fully explained. While Bulosan's Spanish-named "Magno Rubio" brilliantly references his gullibility and the "big blonde" that he can never have (Clarabelle), I encourage a reading practice that will elaborate this transcultural and translingual pun (the "Big Blonde") as structural rather than incidental to Filipino American studies of impairment and to disability studies theories of race. It is interesting to compare this moment of Filipinx Hispanicity with the ways in which it is typically understood in Hispano-Philippines studies. What I mean here is that, unlike Hispanic studies of the Philippines, which have centered Filipino mestizo intellectual production, Magno Rubio's Mexican Spanish does not confer the enlightenment that we witness with turn-of-the-century ilustrados. Instead, Spanish as a signifier shifts meaning within a US racial imaginary. Spanish does not bequeath enlightened subjectivity, but rather becomes an index of the ways in which Filipino and Mexican racialization coincide with the cognitive capacities that racial formation forecloses. Within Bulosan's short story, we see how these differences play out within Filipino migrant communities when Magno asks:

> "Will you help, me Nick?" he asked me suddenly.
>
> "Sure, Magno."
>
> He looked at Claro with displeasure. "Please go away," he told him.
>
> "This illiterate peasant tells me to go away," Claro said contemptuously. "This ignoramus tells a man who has gone to the second grade to go away! Listen, peon—"
>
> "Here's two dollars. Be a gentleman like your uncle."
>
> Claro looked tentatively at the money. He picked up the crisp bills on the table. He grabbed the jug of wine and went to his room.
>
> "What is it, Magno?" I asked.
>
> "I like you to write a letter for me, Nick."
>
> "Where to?"
>
> "My girl in Arkansas."
>
> "I thought you've been writing to her."
>
> "In a way."
>
> "I can't express your feelings, Magno."[17]

Rubio can't read or write; he is disposable and substitutable labor; and his masculinity is dangerous, as he plies his affection toward a white woman. At least, these are the major themes that are explored throughout "Magno Rubio." Magno asks Nick, the narrator, to facilitate his epistolary love affair with his "girl in Arkansas." It is clear from the above scene that Rubio is certainly a savvy and clever negotiator. Nevertheless, notions of racialized stupidity mark his interactions with both Claro and Nick. Nick is perhaps uniquely educated (and perhaps semi-autobiographical, based on Bulosan himself), and thus uniquely positioned in the narrative to compensate for the deficient capacities of Rubio. One of the most intriguing aspects of this scene is the way in which "ignoramus" and "Igorot" are uttered in such close proximity. In the racial imaginaries of Filipino identity, "ignoramus" and "Igorot" highlight an alignment of Philippine indigeneity with ignorance, cognitive deficiency, diminished capacity, illiteracy, and stupidity. Bulosan's story of a Filipino Blonde's cross-racial desire for American white femininity (what Sarita See calls "the clarity of clara") indexes the array of multivalent encounters that the US Borderlands signifies for Filipino American subject formation. Such a resignification of an Asian American cultural text reframes US Latina/o studies along a transpacific axis. In this way, we can elaborate Lonnie Carter's 2003 dramatic reinterpretation of the supposed "moro juramentado" Magno Rubio as a form of new mestizo consciousness, to borrow from Gloria Anzaldúa's formulation. Such a formulation allows us to track what Allan Punzalan Isaac terms the "multiple identificatory and historical markers" of Filipino subjectivity.[18]

Returning to Carter's imaginative re-scripting of the trilingual illiteracy of Rubio, I further argue that, rather than read as epiphenomenal the artifacts of a Filipino migrant "kapaguran" (indolence) and its respite found in a "fantasía amor," we read such an instance as a fundamental rearticulation of Filipino American experience as a transpacific border aesthetic. What does such a translingual archive offer comparative ethnic studies? How does Spanish as a colonial signifier shift meaning in the archipelago and the US-Mexican corridor? Once more, given the illiteracy of Magno Rubio, what can the linguistic capacities undergirding understandings of Filipino racial ambiguity offer disability critique? I push this analysis in an unexpected direction toward the redemption of deficit—the Filipino's historical incapacity to read, speak, and be heard in Spanish; global Hispanism; and US Latina/o studies. Disability theory, I propose, actually allows for such a comparative endeavor. To be sure, there are robust histories of Spanish literacy in Philippine history. Such Hispanic heritage is particularly evident in the historical era known as the "nationalist period" by many Philippine historians.[19] Scholars in Filipino American studies like Allan Punzalan Isaac have gone as far as to ponder on how

> [t]he readings of American texts across the twentieth century are testament to one fact: 7,100 islands did, in fact, float away from Latin American shores to settle for the moment in Asia, only to shuttle back and forth across the Pacific and the Caribbean. Such a critical mass has left a trace

> along the equatorial axis of the Americas. This isthmian connection marking insular tropes and multiple American identities issues from the initial misrecognition of the Philippine archipelago.[20]

The "insular tropes" prompting Philippine "misrecognition" to which Isaac refers render the appellation "Filipino American" a monolithic and immutable "subset descriptor within Asian America."[21] Isaac's critique builds on long-standing debates in Asian American studies that have sought to complexify the subject position of "Asian American" as an "unstable" referent. Indeed, scholars like Martin Manalansan have clarified Asian American "not [as] a universal panethnic identification . . . but rather as the product of the creation of, and engagement with, 'official' categories," pointing to the ways in which "people from different ethnic and national groups are constantly engaged with the discursive formation called Asian America."[22] Such critiques are meant to demonstrate the dangers involved in pegging ethnic studies interventions to US racial projects that have ossified official racial categories, not for the purposes of benign labelling, but rather with the objective of control, power, and discipline. Scholars like Jodi Melamed, Roderick Ferguson, and Chandan Reddy have argued that ethnic studies balkanization and consolidation of monolithic knowledge categories are a pivotal tactic by which the US racial state gets into the business of subjectivity for the ends not of liberation, but of disciplinization.[23] One such effect is the cultural and political appellation of the "model minority," which scholars in Asian American studies have come to understand as serving the interests of white supremacy, rather than as a positive stereotype attesting to the productive assimilation of Asian Americans into US political and social economies. Indeed, simply engaging with the labor histories that inform Carlos Bulosan's "Magno Rubio" immediately challenges the model minority's mythic intellectual capacities. Additionally, this engagement shows the ways in which racial capitalism cannot be easily disentangled from constructions of racialized cognition, as well as the ways in which cognitive capacity is historically tethered to racial capital.

Therefore, invocation of the "Filipino question" in Asian American studies is not to suggest that Filipino American history is unique due to its polysemous nature. Rather, I aim to demonstrate that Asian America's very formation and cultural installation into a US racial imaginary are embedded within racialized notions of cognitive and intellectual ability. This is why Bulosan's illiteracy becomes important for the intersections of race and disability. Moreover, his incapacity to "read the instruments given to him," thus resulting in the miscalculation to "mortgage his future" on the affections of Clarabelle, signifies a non-normativity rooted in colonial anxieties around Filipino sexuality—one that threatens the purity of whiteness because of the specter of miscegenation.[24] Magno Rubio's romance questions the ways in which Asian American history can overwrite the complexities of multiple colonial histories for the understandable yet ultimately insufficient objective of political and scholarly unity.

Rubio's epistolary and illiterate affair challenges Asian American and US empire studies to consider multilingual archives in their explorations of racialized subjectivities and political agency. However, disability studies (alongside the linguistic vacancies of Filipino Hispanic identity) challenge the overly simplistic notion that the access of multilingual archives can be resolved through the acquisition of more languages. Such thinking profits from deficit-based analyses of Filipino histories (if you could just learn Spanish, Filipino America, you could access your true history!). Instead, I claim that exploration of such complex and multivalent racial and linguistic meanings benefit from the framework of transnational feminist disability studies. The kind of postcolonial language politics I advance centers the value of what I call "linguistic deficit" in forging comparative and theoretical connections between Filipino American studies, Latina/o studies, crip theory, and Chicana feminism. Rubio's subprime illiteracy enables a conversation between Filipino American studies and disability theory.

Sarita See, in her article "Gambling with Debt," uses Magno Rubio's illiteracy as an alternative hermeneutic to understand the racial animus that informs criticism of the subprime debtor in the United States after the economic crisis of 2008. This article followed in line with scholarship in critical ethnic studies that sought to understand how the paper-tiger racial specter of irresponsible homebuyers, generally configured racially, alleviated blame from irresponsible lending. Culpability for major financial ruin also trickles down, apparently. Aligning herself with scholarship that calls for the interrogation of "dominant constructions of the subprime debtor," See uses Bulosan's characterization of an illiterate Filipino farmhand who blindly mortgages his future on the unrequited love of Clarabelle to open up space for understanding, as Fred Moten has put it, the "debt that *we* owe the subprime debtor rather than the other way around."[25] Using Magno Rubio as a literary example of the ways in which Filipino diasporic literature has complexified the portrait of political economy by including narratives of migrant labor—in this case, the migrant itinerant labor of the US-Mexican borderscape of California—See presents a perhaps unexpected and important intervention into studies of disability and Filipino subject formation. Migrant Filipino literature challenges the dominant narrative of the "all too familiar refrain" of the "subprime debtor [as] a hapless . . . contractual illiterate whose inability to read the instruments he signed led to the global economic meltdown of 2008." Moreover, "[the subprime] is greedy and tries to cheat the system like her predecessor, the welfare queen."[26]

The subprime is at once a profoundly stupid and a clever immoral cheater. This suggests that the subprime is marked by an implacable incapacity to participate fully in the political economic system that is largely imagined to be co-extensive with liberal meritocratic democracy. This non-assimilability coincides with presumptive and historically sedimented racialized notions of defective cognition and intellectual incapacity ("a hapless . . . contractual illiterate"), pathological family formations ("welfare queen" and Black motherhood), and racialized fear of impurity via miscegenation (Magno Rubio salaciously pursues Clarabelle). Once more, the subprime is constructed as a parasite whose subprime existence is subsisted with state resources—the resources meant for and provided by the sovereign literates. Indeed, she is dependent and ineffectual; her existence is entangled with dominant discourses of racialized stupidity, illiteracy, and cognitive debility—a debility so pernicious, so dangerous, and so toxic that it can push the global economic system into a free fall. I suggest that See's reading of Rubio's illiteracy opens up a productive dialogue between Filipino American studies and discourses around cognitive neurodivergence in disability studies.[27]

See's analysis of Magno Rubio's illiteracy, in my view, potentiates a critical linkage of Filipinx critiques of racial capitalism with disability analysis grounded in destabilizing assumptions around migrant capacity that is not only physical, but also cognitive. Disability studies' "cognitive turn" can articulate productive analyses of the links between historical constructions of both cognition and global racial formations. The critical push in ethnic studies to understand race in a more materialist vein makes it difficult, if morally dubious, to disentangle race from the ways in which it has historically organized asymmetries in distributions of material wealth, resources, and access to the commons.[28] Asymmetries in the political economies of global racial capitalism, I suggest through See's reading, also correspond to the imagined cognitive abilities presumed as a requirement to participate as a robust political and economic subject. Indeed, Bulosan's illiteracy suggests, I argue, that international divisions of labor correspond to intellectual divisions in cognitive capacity. Disability critique pushes critical thought to reexamine the enlightenment presumptions that have historically structured our own perceptions and hierarchical organization of bodily and mental variation from an unspoken, able-bodied, perniciously white male norm that simultaneously configures political economic systems in his favor and benefits from a dyadic construction of racialized debts as both savvy architects of disaster and intellectually deficient.

Certain bodily and cognitive traits can clearly put limitations on mobility, capacity, comfort, and well-being. Feminist disability critiques have challenged social models of the understanding of capacity to keep the particularity of impairment in mind, in order to fully appreciate the materiality of the body. Nevertheless, disability studies has argued that, rather than perceive lack and bodily limitations as de facto deviations from a universal human, such perceptions of lack are socially engineered by virtue of our built-environments and political imaginaries. That is, it is society that produces disability by assigning a social value to bodily variation. The discourse around lack and rehabilitation is also ever-present in racial discourses of the subprime.

*American Son* places the problematics of racial mixture, comparative racialization, and syncretic masculinities at the forefront in disentangling the logics of a US racial imaginary along the US-Mexican corridor. Roley does not present the narrative of an Asian American ascending into respectability via the reparative trajectory of popular minority fiction. Such narratives have been curiously dubbed by Asian American literary critic David Palumbo-Lui "narratives of ethnic healing." Palumbo-Lui has argued that assimilation narratives are rife with an Asian American protagonism debilitated by the individual's "eccentric ethnicity." Ethnicity and race are the obstacles that are presented to be overcome in order to properly assimilate into a respectable, economically stable, and high-achieving minority subject. The perversion of the Asian immigrant is rehabilitated into a figure that is a hallmark of Asian assimilation into the United States: the model minority—a figure that is seemingly endowed with a boundless cognitive capacity and intellectual excellence, and that speaks not particularly to show the merits of Asian culture, but rather to transcend it. Palumbo-Liu has critiqued this brand of minority fiction popularized in the 1990s as being for the benefit of a normative readership to demonstrate that the American Dream works.

But we can also add to Palumbo-Liu's critique: for the benefit of the normative readership that Palumbo-Liu's argument centers in his critique of ethnic assimilation narratives is also crucially a normate readership. Indeed, the articulation of disability with ethnic dilemmas is actually quite striking and more commonplace in much canonical Asian American fiction. For instance, *China Boy* by Gus Lee narrates the story of a Chinese family that relocates to a 1940s San Francisco ghetto, fleeing a post-Communist-revolution China.[29] The protagonist, Kai Ting, is described as having severely limited eyesight, an impairment that exposes him to the economic and physical harm constitutive of anti-Asian and anti-immigrant racism. Amy Tan's *The Kitchen God's Wife* revolves not only around Asian American assimilation, but also coming out as a disabled person. Aunt Helen, who suffers from a malignant brain tumor, urges Pearl, the protagonist, to confess her multiple sclerosis to her mother, Winnie, before Helen dies.[30] Or, as evidenced in the following extract from Carlos Bulosan's canonical example of Filipino American migrant literature, *America Is in the Heart*, which demonstrates the dangers of itinerant labor:

> For a time[,] Carlos lived in Los Angeles with Chris. Fortunately[,] each had an older brother and the two brothers managed to get enough work to keep the four of them alive. Carlos was not well and Chris had lost part of a leg trying to catch a freight train out of Bakersfield . . . Chris, with his wooden leg, and Carlos, with his limp, were able to get a little work now and then, mostly as dishwashers. For long periods, Chris tells me, they lived on pig head . . . and free mackerel from San Pedro, along with seven-cent coffee and doughnuts. In 1936, Carlos was taken to the Los Angeles County Hospital where he underwent three operations for a lesion in his right lung. In all he spent two years in the hospital, most of the time in the convalescent ward. When he finally emerged, on June 7, 1938, his doctor said to him: "You have no more ribs on your right side, young man. But you will live for a while, *Mabuhay!*[31]

Nevertheless, *American Son* is eccentrically ethnic in quite a different way than that articulated in Asian American fiction. Tomas seeks to embody the idealized and troubled masculine subjectivity of a Los Angeleno Mexican gangster known widely as, perhaps ironically in this analysis, a Crip. The narrative is told through the eyes of his younger brother Gabe, whose coming of age is funneled through the various (dis)identifications he has with his brother, Tomas, mainly due to his queerness. Roley recuperates, at least in part, the convergent historical trajectories implicit in Mexican and Filipino experience.

## Linguistic Incapacity: Crip Analysis of Borderlands Multilinguality

I gesture toward a postcolonial crip analysis of the multilinguality of the US-Mexican Borderlands through what I am claiming as a Filipino disability analytic of "linguistic incapacity."[32] However, rather than affirmative comparative literary projects that seek out shared languages or compare across national literatures, I highlight Filipino American/Latino cross-cultural encounters that thematize linguistic loss. Such a topic has been covered in US Latino cultural production, particularly that of Latina authors. For instance, Julia Álvarez's *How the Garcia Girls Lost Their Accents*, Esmeralda Santiago's *Cuando Era Puertorriqueña*, and, most relevant to the present analysis, Gloria Anzaldúa's *Borderlands: The New Mestiza = La Frontera*.[33] My study differs, as I take on linguistic loss of Spanish from a Philippine perspective, where the relationship to Spanish imperialism is markedly different. Literary scholars like John D. Blanco, Adam Lifshey, and John Phelan have all attested to the ways in which Spanish linguistic colonization of the Philippines did not follow in the same paths that saw the eventual Hispanophonization of Latin America. One could argue that no Spanish is there to recover for diasporic Filipino subjects. Linguistic loss for these former Asian denizens of Spanish empire deals with an unrecoverable linguistic capacity to articulate Hispanic identity. Spanish is an absent presence.

The linguistic incapacity of the Filipino when prompted to speak Spanish highlights the ways in which Spanish colonial history and the Spanish language itself are absent presences in Filipinx American studies. Additionally, this incapacity interrogates another avenue of comparative work (US and Spanish imperialisms) that could be engaged by comparative Latinx and Filipinx studies. US empire studies has historiographically used the Philippines as a case study to materialize its critical apparatus. The US's transpacific expansion into Asia marks a significant and, seemingly, sudden shift in the identity of the United States as a global power. Naturally, this expansion neither can nor should be separated from the US's mandate of Manifest Destiny, whereby the acquisition of Mexican territories facilitated the historical development, capitalist accumulation, and philosophical rationalization of eventual transpacific expansion—Spain moved eastward and the US westward, placing the Mexican Borderlands and the Philippine archipelago on a collision course. I center the linguistic trajectories of these competing imperialisms as they emerge in Filipino-Chicano fiction. Such a collision also allows us to revisit a foundational postcolonial feminist question. How do we answer whether the subaltern can speak in peasant, Flip Spanish when the question of Philippine Spanish is itself to contend with its absent presence? Such tensions between power, language, discourse, and subjectivity have been live ideas in postcolonial thought. I ponder the ways that "Filipinx Spanish" is in conversation with the perennial question of whether the subaltern can speak or not.

Centering a conversation between Michel Foucault and Gilles Deleuze, postcolonial theorist Gayatri Spivak is preoccupied with the ways in which international political economy and Western intellectual production are intertwined. She claims that their co-constitution crystallizes a sovereign subject as the opaque center of power and discourse. The production of knowledge and unspoken assumptions around cognitive capacity, drawing on Spivak's framework, are not separate from the hyperextraction of surplus value from human labor. The hyperextractive underside of the Western intellectual has a crucial gender valence; the bodies that perform labor, as Lisa Lowe has argued, enter and circulate into hierarchical relations of production as a result of the ways in which they are categorized via race and gender. Thus, for Lowe, the relations to the modes of production are always "racialized gendered relations."[34] Scholarship on Philippine migration has also tracked the ways in which gender affects export labor economics. For instance, Rhacel Parreñas studies the ways in which racialized gendered relations of production, English language ability, and asymmetrical economics funnel Filipina women largely into domestic work—a topic I will elaborate upon further below.[35] For now, Spivak's "Can the Subaltern Speak?" establishes how the post/colonial intellectual's assertion of intellectual capacity within the framing of Western Enlightenment is inseparable from Western economic interests:

> Let us now move to consider the margins (one can just as well say the silent, silenced center) of the circuit marked out by this epistemic violence, men and women among the illiterate peasantry, the tribals, the lowest strata of the urban subproletariat. According to Foucault and Deleuze (in the First World, under the standardization and regimentation of socialized capital, though they do not seem to recognize this) the oppressed, if given the chance . . . and on the way to solidarity through alliance politics . . . *can speak and know their conditions*. We must now confront the following question: On the other side of the international

> division of labor from socialized capital, inside *and* outside the circuit of the epistemic violence of imperialist law and education supplementing an earlier economic text, *can the subaltern speak?* (Emphasis in original.)[36]

Lamenting the ways in which conservative Western philosophies ignore the question of desire in their critiques of ideology, Spivak elaborates how "the intellectual within socialized capital, brandishing concrete experience, can help consolidate the international division of labor."[37] Spivak argues that conceptions of "desire" become orthodox, para-subjective, and undifferentiated in favor of the "schematic" institutional advancement of ideology as a category of Foucaultian analysis. That is, assuming a monolithic interiority (or a simplistic and interchangeable notion of desire), philosophy can sidestep the question of difference in favor of a master narrative about how power operates globally.[38]

Ideological analysis, therefore, becomes "schematic" rather than "textual"—so archives like literature as articulating differentiated modes of desire, subjugation, and subjectivity are lost in Western philosophy's pathological attachment to an unnamed and tacitly paternalistic "sovereign subject." This subject allows the Euramerican theorist to install himself in the assumption of his cognitive superiority. Therefore, the international division of labor that shapes global political economy mimics and reifies a cognitive division of capacity of who has the authority or ability to be a knowledge producer. This dialectic between the intellectual and the economic is why the subaltern cannot speak, and is instead spoken for or about, in Spivak's schema. There exist (at least within the realms of philosophical discourse in which Spivak traffics) no models that can capture differentiated desires and subjectivity. This is why the third-world woman as subject is inarticulate; she cannot speak.

What was and continues to be innovative about Spivak's critique of Western knowledge production (and, more deliberately, the Westernization of third-world knowledge production) is that she strives to theorize subjectivity, experience, and desire within and as features of the relations to the modes of production. What this means for my purposes is that the class subject cannot be ethically represented as "dispersed" and "dislocated." For Spivak, this dislocation arises from the international division of labor as it is constituted by an international division of intellectual capacity. To wit, she writes:

> In the face of the possibility that the intellectual is complicit in the persistent constitution of the Other as the Self's shadow, a possibility of

> political practice for the intellectual would be to put the economic "under erasure," to see the economic factor as irreducible as it reinscribes the social text, even as it erased, however imperfectly, when it claims to be the final determinant or the transcendental signified.[39]

The modes of "socialized capital" that intellectual capacity emblematizes, according to Spivak, are not simply an ethereal philosophical relation. Rather, they always correspond to international divisions of labor, relations to the modes of production, and, once more, relations to the modes of intellectual production, which presupposes a threshold cognitive capacity—a threshold which is colonially defined. I argue for this re-reading of Spivak's critique of post/colonial reason, given her vexed relationship to Foucaultian historicism. For now, I wish to show how queer of color critique in Filipino history demonstrates an equally skeptical view, contributing to a portayal of colonialism as also inscribing an international division of cognition. In past chapters, I have demonstrated how Philippine historiographical critiques of US "benevolent assimilation" articulate a cognitive history of race and empire. Here, I demonstrate how, in what Victor Román Mendoza elaborates as the "colonianormative," racial-sexual governance materializes through deep-seated ideas around the cognitive capacities of the Philippine autochthonous subject.[40]

Spivak most clearly diverges from the schematic historicist approaches to institutional power. On a cursory reading of this passage—a central point on reading imperialism as being within or outside of Foucaultian biopolitics—we can see her main intervention is identifying the palimpsestic trace of the colonial other that is not only a marginal consideration in the philosophical construction of the subject, but also the underlying substrate upon which subjectivity is even imaginable for the project of knowledge production proper:

> The clearest available example of such epistemic violence is the remotely orchestrated, far-flung, and heterogeneous project to constitute the colonial subject as Other. This project is also the asymmetrical obliteration of the trace of that Other in its precarious Subject-ivity. It is well known that Foucault locates epistemic violence, a complete overhaul of the epitome, in the redefinition of sanity at the end of the European eighteenth century. But what if that particular redefinition was only a part of the narrative of history in Europe as well as in the colonies? What if the two projects of epistemic overhaul worked as dislocated and unacknowledged parts of a vast two-handed engine? Perhaps it is no more than to ask that

> the subtext of the palimpsestic narrative of imperialism be recognized as "subjugated knowledge," "a whole set of knowledges that have been disqualified as inadequate to their task or insufficiently elaborated: naive knowledges, located low down on their hierarchy, beneath the required level of cognition or scientificity."[41]

Spivak brings these questions back to the act of speech or, more deliberately, to those discursive maneuvers that reach the threshold of knowledge production. Spivak allows for a reckoning not only of the ways in which Enlightenment is one of the ideological mechanisms justifying and advancing an international division of labor, but also of the ways in which such divisions of labor correspond to divisions of cognitive ability. What is productive about Spivak's critique of Western Enlightenment reason is that it centers the act of speech in articulating claims that can not only be heard, but that can reach the threshold of adding to the field of human knowledge.

Such power/knowledge, speech, and subjective issues find more political and optimistic resolution in Chicana feminist theories around linguistic sovereignty. In the previous section, I demonstrated the extant articulations between Asian Americanist cultural critique and disability frameworks that have constituted narratives of ethnic assimilation. The current section draws on Spivak's critique of postcolonial reason and the incapacity of the third world woman to speak, to advance a Filipino American race and gender analysis of the question of Philippine Spanish—a conversation prompted by the debilitating valences of peasant, Flip Spanish in the US-Mexican Borderlands as advanced in *American Son*. In the next section, I attempt to show how the "linguistic incapacity" signified by Flip Spanish can actually animate comparative ethnic studies convergences and unforeseen filiations between Filipinx and Chicanx studies.

What does subaltern speech look like in a Filipinx rendition of the US Borderlands? In which language does it materialize? What sorts of commentaries does it enable on the social and political organization of racial capitalism? To arrive at an answer to these questions means contending with the ways that Roley's *American Son* manifests a genre of anti-assimilation that entangles with the question of pathological Spanish. Pathological here has two meanings. The first is the disruption of the respectable, model minority Asian American subject—a disruption that I suggest transpires through a cross-racial identification with Chicano masculinity. For the Filipino-Chicano subject, this ethnic masculine attachment becomes a question of labor. Roley's perverse Filipino subject,

Tomas, who "is the son who helps pay the mortgage by selling attack dogs to rich people and celebrities," is also:

> the son who causes . . . embarrassment by showing up at family parties with his muscles covered in gangster tattoos and his head shaved down to stubble and his eyes bloodshot from pot. He is really half white, half Filipino but dresses like a Mexican, and it troubles our mother that he does this. She cannot understand why if he wants to be something he is not he does not at least try to look white.[42]

His Mexican appearance, his white Pontiac, and skinscripted Virgen de Guadalupe tattoo all give Tomas professional credibility in the eyes of his white Hollywood clientele. He arrives at the house of a potential customer who is interested in purchasing an attack dog. The neighborhood, unnamed, is renowned for being populated by famous people. Arriving with the client at the house, Tomas

> stops and lowers his window before a white intercom perched on a metal stand. Tomas pushes a red button. We wait. He tries again and after a minute a lady's voice that sounds Mexican—probably the maid—asks what we want.
>
> We've come to sell some dogs, he says into the box.
>
> Again, the sound of static. Then the crackled voice comes on and says they don't take solicitors.
>
> No, listen, Tomas says. We have the dogs with us now.
>
> We no take solicitations, it says.
>
> Then the static clicks off.
>
> Tomas frowns and hits the side of the intercom and presses the button. I already talked to the señor of the casa, he says to the voice when it comes on again.
>
> You speak to him already?
>
> Sí.
>
> There is a pause, and then the voice says *okay* and the gate swings open. Its iron bottom scrapes along the driveway. You'd think they'd get a faster motor if they can afford a house like this, he says.
>
> That was really great Spanish, Tomas, I say.
>
> Fuck you, he says.[43]

The "probable maid" is literally the gatekeeper. Through the intercom, the act of speech takes on a special significance vis-à-vis the scopic cross-racial imaginaries that *American Son* attends to. In this moment, the visual racial signifiers that would readily attach to Tomas's stylized self-presentation obviously cannot obtain. Therefore, Spanish becomes the mode through which access can be secured. Tarrying on the question of Spanish, we can surmise that its use at the gates of a palatial Californian mansion is to forge a minority affinity between himself and the speaker of accented English. However, in this interaction, Tomas does not intend to speak across racial lines, but rather to speak downward. Tomas cites the authority of the "señor of the casa," implicitly signaling a power dynamic in which she is clearly on the bottom, as she is "probably the maid" by narrative admission. Obviously, Tomas's linguistic stylings do not reach the level of a robust exchange. As this interaction is articulated within Asian American literature, Tomas's admittedly feeble use of "really great Spanish" (corroborated by his vitriolic response to Gabe's compliment) foreshadows an eventual linguistic breakdown—his racial performative of Mexican masculinity undercut by an anxious use of Spanish. What I want to highlight is the comparative interaction between two racial and gendered laboring bodies extant in the US Mexican borderscape: the ethnic masculine purveyor of guard dogs and the Mexican "maid." The former's visual identification is hampered by defective Spanish, while the latter is racially identified solely through accented English: "a lady's voice that sounds Mexican." Race, gender, and imaginaries around which bodies perform what labors come to a head inside the Hollywood mansion. Lucinda, "probably the maid," asks:

> "Ustedes son hermanos?
>
> [Tomas] looks like he doesn't understand but doesn't want her to know this.
>
> She wants to know if we're brothers, I tell him.
>
> I know that.
>
> He glares at me and I shut up, but she faces me now and expects an answer.
>
> Sí.
>
> Yo creo que no.
>
> I nod. Mi madre tampoco lo cree.
>
> She bites her lip and thinks a moment.
>
> Se parecen por la forma de sus ojos, she says, and then turns to Tomas: You do not seem so. But I can tell it in the shape of your eyes.[44]

In Lucinda's home, we note a rift forming between the brothers along linguistic and racial lines. Lucinda's curiosity as to the familial status of the brothers stems from the simple fact that Gabe, the Filipino in the scene who actually can speak Spanish for reasons not substantiated in the novel, possesses white mestizo features. Tomas, however, is dark, like their mother, which renders possible in this context the misrecognition that his ethnic masculine performance of Mexicanness relies upon. The scene features the linguistic breakdown of Tomas—he is not up to the linguistic task of robust communication with the maid. Gabe's interpretative interventions painfully render clear the pretext of Tomas's performative act, which is later corroborated by the bilingual exchange/translation that Lucinda provides at the end of the above passage.

Undercutting Tomas's racial performative is not solely his lack of Spanish. The reader is invited to understand this linguistic incapacity through how his younger brother's effeminacy juxtaposes his own consistent access to Latino masculinity. In the scene above, it is evident that the white mestizo-looking Gabe has the ability to converse with Lucinda. I want to highlight that, in this scene, the "maid" creates a language space wherein critical questions around normative ethnic masculinity can be questioned, reformulated, and disturbed. This falls in line with the binaristic modes of border thinking around gender, race, and sexuality that a "conciencia mestiza" would promote. Indeed, the novel's opening posits the juxtaposition of the bildungen of the brothers as a question of racialized sexuality. Fearing his brother would undermine his credibility as an attack dog salesman/gangster, Tomas inveighs to Gabe: "If the client sees you standing there like that he's gonna think you're my houseboy."[45] We begin with the Chicano-Filipino subject whose attachments to racialized criminal masculinity are rendered evident. Meanwhile, the narrative voice that articulates these attachments is rendered a houseboy. The subject voice that prompts exploration of multiracial, multilingual, and cross-racial articulations is that of the queer Asian American subject. This juxtaposition is further complicated by the discourses of mixed race that come to adumbrate Filipino racial identity and embodiment. The question of how Spanish, or its absent presence, is implicated in the comparative racialization of Filipinos and US Latinos must also contend with how gender and sexuality continually inform how Filipino bodies become scripted into rubrics of ethnic masculinity and Orientalist femininity. I say this because, indeed, while not evident in the excerpted scene, equally undercutting of Tomas's racial performative is not only the language abilities to which Gabe apparently has access (coupled with his trace of white mestizo features), but also Gabe's putative queerness. The ways in which these masculinities interact is presented in *American Son* as a question of labor—an analysis I will return to below. Nevertheless, the articulation of

Gabe's bildung alongside Tomas's pathological ethnic masculinity invokes the specter of comparative racialization through a familiar gendered and sexual trope in Orientalist discourses. This is what scholars in queer Asian American studies have called the prototypical Asian American bottom.[46] By novel's end, Gabe completes his transformation into gangster, like his brother, through an act of violence and theft. What was articulated as a juxtaposition of Latino masculinity with Asian effeminacy transforms into an anti-assimilationist trajectory from Asian bottom to Latino top.

Roley's *American Son* maps the trajectory of Gabe's development clearly—along the crip assimilationist trajectory into cross-racial criminality, rather than toward the upstanding model minority or ilustrado. Gabe, throughout the novel, is represented as the son that can be saved from the perverse criminal influences of the Los Angeles Borderlands. His model minority Asianness, normative white features, and intellectual excellence are marked as sites of normate uplift into the American Dream that his mother's family desires for him. He is enrolled in a private, mostly white school for high achieving students; he actually helps his mother around the house; his kind, passive, and mild-mannered disposition is much more consonant with how Asians are configured in American culture. Gabe's characterization is functionalized as making his brother Tomas's anomalous performances of criminal masculinity all the more aberrant. Nevertheless, the Borderlands landscape seems to prevail in perverting the normate development of even Gabe into a respectable subject. He steals Tomas's white Pontiac. The grand theft auto takes the reader into the desert where Gabe's newfound, if implicit, racial reorientations are stunningly subverted by the queerness of his sexuality.

As the novel establishes, in order for Tomas to effectively profit from his career as a guard dog breeder, he must embody prevailing racialized fantasies of Mexican ethnic masculinity and criminality—what a US racial imaginary discursively stereotypes and what the novel portrays as the Cholo gangster. Roley accurately and strategically presents this racial drag whose effeminized foil is the Filipinx femme bottom racially castrated by Orientalist fantasies that construct the West as top.[47] Such a feminine foil is established by the ways in which Tomas homophobically reads the masculinity of his brother Gabe, the bildung protagonist and narrator, via the trope of "houseboy." The Asian American bottom is the most abject form of racial identification in the US Borderlands. Gabe constructs the internal narrativization of his racial anxiety around his sexuality and gender. Such anxiety is displayed during Gabe's first rebellious act of stealing Tomas's car and selling his prized dog. When the white Pontiac station wagon is towed, the reader is subjected to a long dialogue between Gabe and an older white male tow truck driver, Stone, who Gabe subtly suspects racializes and genders him as what Victor Román Mendoza calls the "Filipino bottom," or what Eng-Beng Lim dubs the "native boy."[48] The narrative subverts reader expectation of the truck driver's racial-sexual turpitude when the hotel that is booked for Gabe is actually arranged by Gabe's mother:

> [Stone] unbuttons his shirt further, then peels back the damp fabric to reveal more of his chest. Matted chest hair clings to the shirt wool, then pops back. It seems weird that he would do this, and I look down.[49]

The Filipino bottom averts Stone's gaze, not wanting to be conscripted into the inevitable Orientalist fantasy of the native boy. Gabe likes the attention, as "[Stone] looks upon me with fatherly concern. An overwhelming warmth spreads within me like an intake of hot sour breath. Blushing, I turn away."[50] The scene between these two proceeds in this fashion: Gabe's Asian body attracts the white sexualizing stare of Stone, which Gabe attempts to avoid. As Gabe notices Stone's "matted chest hair," the truck driver invites him to

> Look here, he says
>
> There is a quarter-sized red scar on his chest, and suddenly he takes my hand in his sweaty palm and leads my finger to it. I have to force myself not to jerk away, this is so surprising. His black chest hair feels thick against my fingertip, the skin warm. A pulse beats. Though I do not know whether it is his or mine.[51]

The trace of the ilustrado here can actually be read as a queer presence that Gabe's bildungen centers as part of his racial sexual development. I suggest that the interaction above is a fundamental turning point in *American Son* for trading the Oriental perversity of bottomhood for the pathology of racialized sexuality. The possibility of an erotic encounter haunts Stone's and Gabe's interaction without ever fully materializing. Gabe's racialized sexuality in the scene above produces a racial and gendered misrecognition rooted in two seemingly disparate and yet complimentary formations. The first is the sexual economy of Orientalism that shapes desires and the articulation of racialized bodies that inhabit them. The second is the racialized and gendered landscape of the Borderlands, which also conditions Filipinx embodiment and identity. In Roley's novel these disparate and yet co-constructing formations of the Borderlands and Orientalism manifest in the linguistic politics of Filipinx Spanish, as was analyzed in the interactions between Tomas, Gabe, and Lucinda ("the maid").

Racial/gendered labor in the US Mexican Borderlands overlays the question of Flip, peasant Spanish. The reader sees that Tomas's acts of dissimulation end in eventual and embarrassing misrecognition when he asks the "Mexican maid" during his sales pitch to the man of the house: "Hey do you think you could get us a glass of water or something? . . . It's getting hot in here."[52] Gabe "stiffens" at this request (another speech act gone awry), as he is able to intuit the "real" status of Lucinda as "not the maid," to which Tomas feigns acknowledgment. This climaxes in physical violence at the end of the extended scene:

> His knuckles hit me hard . . . salty blood floods my mouth . . . the concrete meet[s] my temple . . .
>
> Don't you fucking talk disrespect to me [says Tomas].
>
> I wasn't disrespecting you [says Gabe].
>
> Don't you overstand me with your Flip, peasant Spanish! [shouts Tomas][53]

I suggest that this eruption of violence finds its origin, however, in the foundational misrecognition of Lucinda as maid. This misrecognition is also a recognition of the ways in which racialized gendered conceptions of labor attach to the bodies of women of color in the Borderlands. Here, Spanish plays a crucial role. Her linguistic access is one of the mechanisms through which Tomas is revealed to be a fraud. However, it is also one of the racial signifiers that configures Latina bodies as disposable and interchangeable forms of racialized domestic labor. I pose the question of the enduring absent presence of Spanish in Filipino America in order to articulate the problematic of Hispanophone linguistic capacity to subalternist postcolonialism, as introduced above through Spivak's meditations on subaltern speech acts. The rubric of comparative racialization and the gendered-sexual tropes that such comparison simultaneously challenges and solidifies, I suggest, should not be disarticulated from the figure that can, indeed, speak Spanish but is rendered silent—Lucinda. While Tomas's and Gabe's relationship to power is presented as still in flux because of the ambiguities of racial error that inhere within assimilation, Lucinda's misrecognition as maid constitutes a parasubjective silencing of women of color in narratives in and around the border. *American Son* invites us to be attentive to the subaltern woman of color who rarely figures within questions of Philippine Hispanicity at all, except as a racial-sexual-gender trope of idealized or stereotyped womanhood.

For this reason, I move to a reading of the Chicana feminist thought of Gloria Anzaldúa, who has quite assiduously attended to the problems of subaltern speech of women of color. Chicana feminist analysis is a vital site that can shed light on the connections between linguistic sovereignty and the linguistic incapacity that I have been suggesting attaches to the Philippine Hispanic. This postcolonial crip critique of linguistic incapacity dialogues productively with Chicana feminist affirmations of linguistic sovereignty foundational to Gloria Anzaldúa's *Borderlands*. In it, Anzaldúa argues for the preservation of multiple Spanishes that would be deemed both defective by a US Anglophone racial imaginary and derivative or an aberration by the vanguards of Hispanophone linguistic integrity: *La Real Academia de la Lengua Española* (The Royal Academy of the Spanish Language). Her chapter, "To Tame a Wild Tongue," is an inventory of defective Spanishes, and the inevitable miscommunications that arise under the linguistic normativities of the English and Castilian Spanish, as these languages underwrite the multiple imperialisms of the Borderlands. However, while the language of defect, or anomalous Spanish, does inform the articulation of a conciencia mestiza, the deployment of mestiza consciousness productively evades a deficit-based critique of linguistic normalization that obtains in cultural nationalist worldviews. The "wild tongues" of defective Spanish (or "los del español deficiente") cannot be tamed. Rather, they are "cut out"—thus combining the physical realities of language-making with the psychic realities of language maintenance. Anzaldúa lists the various tongues and linguistic media she *can* communicate in as (not in spite of being) a Chicana *tejana*. Such a listing strategy has the effect of diversifying the landscape of language encounters within Latina/o, Chicana/o, and Hispanic identity.

The insistence on capacity, instead of defect (or, rather, compromised heritage as enabling of different kinds of ability or novel interactions with the environment), is corroborated through the common linguistic act of codeswitching. Rejecting the assumption that words borrowed from English are an "agringado" distortion of Spanish labeled as "anglicisms," "pochismos," and the "pachuco tongue," Anzaldúa affirms that she "may switch back and forth from English to Spanish in the same sentence or in the same word."[54] She stresses that the cognitive landscape for those of hybrid linguistic identities is different from that of a monolingual normative culture, which predicates itself on linguistic uniformity, rather than diversity. Indeed, such hybrid language moves are not de facto perversions of the purity of English and Spanish (undoubtably the most pervasive colonial languages historically), both of which mastheaded the spread of Spanish, American, and British colonialisms globally. Rather, they represent the articulation of different kinds of linguistic capacities within the constrained field of agency of imperialism, as it has constructed the subjectivities of those residing in the US-Mexican Borderlands.

Anzaldúa insists that we must understand the proliferation of defective Spanishes and Chicano identity as part of "250 years of Spanish/Anglo colonization," which has "developed significant differences in the Spanish we speak."[55] "Defective" in this itinerary means seemingly substandard, low-brow, and mangled forms of Spanish that do not conform to the Spanish of Cervantes and Spain. Indeed, many of the regional Spanishes that have preserved the "archaisms" of "Medieval Spanish" cannot be detached from the conquest of New Spain initially and famously given impetus by the long egoistic shadow of Hernán Cortés.[56] A mestiza consciousness is a Chicana feminist dialectic that preserves sovereignty, not through coherence, but through bifurcation, hybridity, and mixture. The deficient Spanish of Chicana border thought attends to the ways in which imperialism proliferates racial, gendered, and sexual oppression that a flexible conciencia mestiza (with deficient Spanish) can navigate. In Filipino America, we can see the palimpsestic traces of the vexed linguistic landscape of Spanish imperialism through its relationship to US Latina/os. Indeed, such obvious yet undertheorized comparative affinities demand the feminist flexibility of Chicana mestiza consciousness.

## Filipinx Spanishes: Crip Comparative Race Analysis

The multiple languages of the imperial history of the Philippines present a dynamic and complex interaction of Filipino racialization in the United States, as it intersects with the racialization of Mexican Americans. Filipino American literature already testifies to the instability and multivalence of the category "Asian American" by thematizing, among other issues, linguistic syncretism and hybridity. In other contemporary work, the thematic of Filipino/Mexicano borderscapes is further articulated as a compelling comparative frame to understanding overlapping colonial histories of the Spanish and US empires. I understand this overlap as another such understudied Borderlands, which I thematize by centering the figure of what I call the "castrated mestizo." Through this figure, which Roley claims as an "American son," I seek to explain the ways in which masculinity and effeminacy interact within the field of racial embodiment in the comparative racial projects of Filipinoness and Latinoness. I argue that, in order to fully apprehend the multivalent embodiment and racial error that circumscribe the misrecognition of Filipinos within global understandings of Hispanicity (in this case, US Latino studies), we must pursue comparative race theory alongside feminist disability—a move that I call "crip comparative race analysis." The castrated mestizo represents the intersection of Chicano and Filipino embodiment. Within the analytical structure of disabled femininity that I have articulated throughout this book, I attempt to understand the polysemous Filipino body—whose provenance is a "Hispanic Asia"—through the optic of Chicana feminist theory. This inevitably leads me to the question of Flip Spanish—a wild tongue that is not characterized by the preservation of Spanish but rather through its absent presence, a condition I term "linguistic incapacity." The comparative space of Filipino/Latino America is where we can reorient some of the foundational claims to linguistic coherence and sovereignty outlined in *Borderlands*. For this reason, the anti-assimilation narrative of *American Son* invites intersectional comparative readings that are attentive to the ways in which heteromasculinity informs the interpretation of racial error, (mis)recognition, and the imperial patchwork of Hispanic American colonialisms.

The comparative raciality and affinities between Filipinos and Latinos in a US borderscape do not stop at the analogical. In fact, comparative race projects intervene in the ways in which US racial systems have propagated racial regulations through analogy. Speaking in this context, Hsuan L. Hsu argues that the methodological insight of comparative race studies is uncovering the ways that "literature can articulate tensions between different racial groups . . . [in order to] critique processes of comparative racialization without reproducing their logic of analogy."[57] Therefore, we see that the affinities shared by the Filipino and Latino body gain meaning in shared colonial histories as partially the products of both Spanish and US imperial projects. While the Philippines is a far-off nation in American transpacific expansion, I consider the Filipino as part, however provisional, of the US-Mexican Borderlands. What new understandings can we come to by theorizing Filipino American subjectivity through the frame of feminist border studies?

Naturally, this kind of project is incredibly problematic, relying on damaging assumptions around Asian embodiment and classist stereotypes of Mexican identity as deviant, gangster, and violent. We, however, cannot come to such an understanding of the deviant masculinity of Mexicanidad unless we assume the effeminate ineffectuality of the Filipino as agentive subject. Thus, the robust ethnic masculinity of the Chicano gains meaning through the castration of Asian America, while the normativity of whiteness endures.

"Linguistic incapacity" is a state of becoming wherein you are not able to speak in the language that your body looks like. Part of reading the dynamics of linguistic colonialism centering the body wrests discourse and power away from the realm of the abstract and into that of physical and cognitive ability. The Filipino is confronted with an archive that is their history written in a colonial language that precludes access. Such is, I argue, a perennial tension at the heart of Philippine nationalist historiography. The famous political figures of the anti-colonial Enlightenment we identify with are bodies that stand in for a national body—until we get to the tongue. Extending this tension into the Mexican American Borderlands, we see an iteration of this dynamic of "not being able to speak in the language that you look like," with racial errors constitutive of Latino-Filipino comparative racialization. The character of Tomas, confronted with who he believes to be the Mexican maid, is prompted to speak in the language that his drag demands—proving that the Filipino and Mexican are not self-same, and undercutting the ethnic masculinity meant to amend the castration that Asian American queer theory argues is constitutive of Asian racialization.

To the casual observer, it might seem strange to use Filipino American literature, Anglophone as it is, as the medium through which to understand the existence of a thoroughly improper Filipino Spanish; that is precisely the point. This is remarkable, as Filipino American affinity with Spanish actually upends the political commitments and energies that suffuse the mestizo bourgeois nationalism at the heart of Philippine Enlightenment. Gestures to shed light on the Hispanization of the Filipino have been met with uneven and inevitably classist dimensions, as we might see with the perhaps disproportionate presence of Hispanic culture in Jessica Hagedorn's *Dogeaters* as representative of a unified Filipino culture. I am not interested in recovering Filipino Spanish, as we might see in recuperative gestures reexamining (for instance) the renaissance in the cultural production of Chavacano (Philippine pidgin Spanish). Such dialectical instantiations of Spanish, subtended by Malay grammar and morphology, produce cultural and linguistic vistas that can amend the narrow transatlantic Iberian and Latin American ordering of the global

Hispanic. This direction of analysis is, to be sure, important and vital. It relies on the assumption that the Filipino tongue is, indeed, not lacking, can and does possess Spanish (even in pidgin form), and produces a robust culture that is thriving despite imminent colonial erasures.[58] I do not disagree. However, within the protraction of Hispanic modernities in Filipino America, I seek, instead, to uphold the racial errors, misrecognitions, and linguistic debilities that are necessarily occasioned by the Filipino's *lack* of access to Spanish. I attempt to understand the question of Filipino Spanish within a Filipino American and Latino comparative framework as an epistemological problem that moves disability into the postcolonial. What kinds of "accessible futures," as feminist disability theorist Alison Kafer puts it, can we imagine when linguistic access to a Spanish past reveals the incapacities of Filipinos of the contemporary moment to apprehend a multilingual archive?[59]

Historically undeniable is the reality that the linguistics of colonialism transpired very differently in the Philippines than they did in, say, New Spain[60] and the Mexican American Borderlands. While I would not dispute Philippine Spanish as one among many Spanishes that have been marginalized in our understanding of an impossibly diverse Hispanic world, following along the lines of disability studies critique, I am interested in the wild Filipino tongue that has been cut out and tamed, to invoke Gloria Anzaldúa's famous formulation.[61] Linguistic deficit of Spanish as one of the principal motors of "Hispanization" and therefore "Filipinoness" is, I venture to say, one of the main causes for the dearth of sustained comparative work between Latino studies and Filipino studies as they reflect on Spanish American imperialisms. For the purposes of understanding the comparative racializations of Latino and Filipino bodies, I revel in linguistic deficit—a deficit I argue is constitutive of Filipino subjectivity and its "Hispanic" culture. In other words, it is that which is not there—Spanish through a painfully absent presence—that ironically marks the Filipinos' proximity to histories of Spanish imperialism, thus subsisting a sustained comparative affinity with US Latino scholarship and theory. It is the deficit, the very linguistic incapacity of Flip Spanish, that presents an exciting opportunity to reinvigorate comparative work. I find opportunity in examining Filipino postcolonial subjectivity as a constant construction through the linguistic lack of Spanish—a present absence that I call "linguistic incapacity." Gloria Anzaldúa's glorious "How To Tame a Wild Tongue," which appears in *Borderlands*, takes to task the psychological and bodily harm of linguistic colonialism into English.

This postcolonial crip analytic puts at the forefront questions of (linguistic) access to colonial histories, literatures, and archives written in languages that are not commonly spoken or acquired, due to linguistic strategies of colonization and indigenous language acquisition through the frame of Chicana feminist thought offered by Anzaldúa. Part of my purpose here is to connect Filipino American studies and queer Asian American studies with Chicana feminist thought. Additionally, forging such affinities within the absence of Filipino Spanish articulates comparative ethnic studies within a frame of race and disability. I argue for such connections because implicit questions around language access are simultaneously peripheral and yet, I would suggest, central to the diverse fields of Philippine and Filipino American studies. In Roley's borderscape, the racial drag of the American son, Tomas, collapses the national and cultural signs that would imagine the Philippines and Mexico as discrete spaces.

## Crip/Flip Chicana Feminism and the Domestic Worker/Maid

In *American Son*, we do not have the presentation of the typical Asian American assimilation narrative. Typical assimilation narration presents an eccentrically ethnic protagonist who integrates into social, economic, and political modes of a respectability that simultaneously engulfs such subjects into their ethnic particularity. These kinds of narratives signify for a normative white readership that America works by demonstrating the extent to which Asian Americans can mimic white middle-class existence. Asian Americanist David Palumbo-Liu has critiqued such literatures as narratives of "ethnic healing." The characterization of minority assimilation narratives as being of "healing" is significant for a disability studies optic. Reading disability refracted through a US racial imaginary, we can see that ethnic protagonism is actually a perverse impairment that assimilation is meant to rehabilitate. However, such rehabilitation is not just for an Asian American subject attempting to access the material resources of the good life, which, eventually, ends up being a form of "cruel optimism"—a socialized want or desire for a respectable good existence that paradoxically does harm.[62] Again, the impairments and debilities of race are socially produced as the phenomenological impairments of disability are produced when a body's difference interacts with built environments, political architectures, and representations for which such difference is anathema. The bildungen of Asian assimilation is one such rhetorical architecture, where the sexual, gender, and racial perversity of immigrants is unfurled as impairments to be superseded. The "eccentric" ethnic is the depraved supercrip in narrative protocols of American minority racial integration. The model minority is the neurodivergent, often queer, savant, fueling the inspirational pornographic spectacle of the Asian immigrant who overcomes their linguistic foreignness, racial difference, and sexual/gender strangeness to become a high achiever.

Palumbo-Liu has illuminated that the ethnic healing that rehabilitates difference into whiteness is not for the benefit of the Asian American subject, but rather is a narrative prosthetic constructed for the benefit of a white readership. "Ethnic healing" is a narrative device in dialogue with those critiqued by disability studies known as "narrative prosthesis." Disability studies theorists David T. Mitchell and Sharon L. Snyder's narrative prostheses are representational techniques that are designed to "remove the unsightly from view," normalizing the body through representation.[63] Disability in such narratives serves a cathartic function for the audience that apprehends them. Bodily and mental impairment are construed as "textual obstacles" to be overcome by the normate protagonist. Ethnicity and racial difference become prosthetic devices that circumscribe and solidify the whiteness (read: able-mindedness and able-bodiedness) of the normate American subject.

The articulation of a comparative crip race analytic must contend with feminist disability analytics to ensure racialized gendered discourses of exploitative labor that mark the subjectivities of women of color are not narratives that "fall away" from our critical worldviews. By way of conclusion, I end with the most jarring misrecognition, in which we can apprehend how the uptake of criminal ethnic masculinity is not disconnected from the specter of the subaltern "servant of globalization." In order to understand how to contextualize the linguistic incapacities of the Philippine Hispanic vis-à-vis Latina/o studies within global racial capitalism, I turn to Tomas and Gabe's mother, Ika.

A substantial structuring device of *American Son* is the epistolary relationship between Ika and her brother, Betino. In letters throughout the book, Betino expresses his concern over the racialization of his nephews as Latinos due to the "bad influences of Los Angeles." Often, Betino would encourage Ika to bring her family back to the Philippines, which was "not as bad" as many "expatriate balikbayans" would make it out to be, in order to set the boys on a straight and narrow path. Fearing that Tomas's degeneration is so complete and that his sister Ika is too late in responding to his pleas for correction, Betino writes that "[Tomas] has become a gangster and is in my mind no longer a Filipino . . ."[64] The idea of being a Filipino is heavily class-based for Betino, as he takes up residence in Forbes Park, a very wealthy gated subdivision in Makati, Metro Manila. In an earlier letter, preceding Tomas's Chicano perversion, Betino exclaims how

> with their mestizo looks they would have been very successful with the girls, no doubt, which perhaps can give quiet boys confidence that will leave them with a serenity allowing greater application to their studies. It is a shame you will not send your boys to live with me in Manila. I could teach them the values of education, work, discipline, and respect for their elders and Asian a Spanish heritage.[65]

Tomas and Gabe's "mestizo looks" predict a sexual availability of Filipina girls, thus allowing the boys to embrace their enlightened Asian and Spanish heritage. This sets up a competition with what kind of Hispanic identification is desirable. Forbes Park and Los Angeles offer vastly different prisms through which we can read Filipino mestizaje. In the US Borderlands, racialized criminality pollutes the pristine and erudite kind of Hispanicity that Philippine Enlightenment promises. In this sense, it is assimilation into the US that precludes inheritance of an enlightened subjectivity at the center of nationalist historiographies of Philippine political sovereignty. Interestingly, citation of a Forbes Park-oriented Asian/Spanish heritage contravenes racialized, gendered, and sexualized prisms of a degeneracy that, for Betino, attaches to the Philippines erroneously. He writes to Ika:

> This fetish you seem to have for being an American seems to me quite disconcerting. Filipinos have their problems, of course, many problems, but I can assure you that in fact we have virtues as well. Perhaps some people in other countries may have a low estimation of Filipinos; may I suggest that this is inaccurate, a misperception based on seeing the many poor, uneducated domestic laborers and bar girls who must live abroad to earn money, as you yourself should well know.[66]

Here Betino, I suggest, indicates that it is pathological motherhood that has contributed to this fracturing of the respectable Filipino. At the center of Betino's critique of Ika's obsession with becoming American is indeed the image of the "poor, uneducated domestic laborer" that, in his implication, she partially contributes toward. Ika is one of those "bar girls who must live abroad to earn money" as she "should well know."

Her diasporic status as immigrant contributes to the degeneracy of Tomas and Gabe. It is the pathological Filipina domestic laborer's fracturing of the Filipino boys from their rightful heritage as enlightened mestizos.

Gabe eventually submits to the racial economic worldview that his uncle subscribes to, in which diasporic Filipinas incur a deficit-based understanding of the Philippines in the world—particularly with regard to the subproletarian kinds of work that global capitalism ascribes to them. However, it is not the lens of Asian Hispanicity that informs the classist and misogynist interpretations of Ika's diasporic existence. Rather, Gabe orchestrates a stunning misrecognition at a meal shared by him, his mother, his aunt, and Stone—the truck-driving "white daddy" mentioned above. Because of Gabe's whiteness, he convinces Stone that his white aunt is his mother. Gabe does so to maintain the illusion that he is white. However, in order to explain the presence of Ika's dark skin, he engages Stone: " 'that's our maid,' I say, gesturing towards Mom."[67] Gabe proceeds to pass his white aunt as his real mother. In a painful scene, Ika confronts her son:

> What did you tell him about me? she suddenly says.
> Tell who?
> The tow truck man.
> I pause. Nothing.
> She shakes her head, disappointedly.
> . . . Yes you do, Gabe . . .
> Why was he ignoring me?
> I don't know. Some people can be rude, I've noticed.
> Gabe.
> *What*? I face her, the blood violent in my fists.
> Gabe . . . Did you tell him I was your maid? She says.[68]

Gabe relies on the racial and gendered images of women of color as domestic servants to mislead Stone. In a scene painful to interpret, it becomes evident that Gabe's appraisal of his mother aligns with the pathological misperceptions that his Forbes Park-dwelling uncle lays at Ika's door: she is a "poor, uneducated domestic laborer . . . who must live abroad to earn money." She does not embody the many virtues that Filipinos possess. It is the Filipina as domestic laborer, the Latina as maid, rather than the asymmetrical power relations of transnational capital, that is to blame for the "low estimation of Filipinos" from which Gabe desires distance, leveraging the ambiguities of his "mestizo looks." Ika cannot participate at the table as his mother. She is silenced. She is the domestic worker. She is the maid.

The problematic of racial misrecognition is not uncommon in Filipinx American literature. As this chapter has demonstrated, the geographical and political positioning of the Filipino body in colonial labor regimes has had a prismatic effect on Filipino racialization. In the next chapter, I continue examining this motif of racial misrecognition in Filipino American subjectivity, but pivot from the context of literary fiction. Jose Antonio Vargas's memoir *Dear America: Notes from an Undocumented Citizen* helps to demonstrate the ways that Latinx and Filipinx politics are intimately entwined in Filipino identity formation and even aesthetic politics. My aim with this chapter on *American Son* and the chapter on *Dear America* to follow is to recognize the ways that the racial misrecognitive is not only a subjective moment of productive instability, but also an aesthetic and formal mode of political worldmaking.

# 3 | Filipino Jose, Not Mexican José

## *On the Disability Affects of Filipinx Undocumentality and Racial Dysphoria*

In 2011, Jose Antonio Vargas published a watershed essay in the *New York Times Magazine* in which he confessed to being an undocumented immigrant. It was a confession that shook the nation, as Vargas was a famous and successful journalist, awarded the Pulitzer Prize for his contributions to coverage of the 2007 Virginia Tech shooting. In his self-exposé, he describes how, at the age of thirteen, he was involuntarily and unknowingly sent to the United States with a coyote by his mother. He discovered a few years later that his documentation (a Permanent Resident Card, also known informally as a "Green Card") was falsified, only when he attempted to get a driver's license. Feeling betrayed, confused, and afraid, he lived with the secret knowledge that he was not supposed to be in the United States, at least insofar as his legal status was concerned. He followed up this disclosure with his Pulitzer Prize-winning memoir *Dear America: Notes of an Undocumented Citizen* in 2018, fleshing out more so the details of his life, his troubled identification as an activist, and the networks of support that sustained him. I am compelled to engage with Vargas's work and life-writing as an immigrant rights activist (even though this is a term with which he acknowledges an uneasy relationship), and as a mouthpiece for the undocumented immigrant community in the United States. One important rhetorical tactic that he implements is to normalize the reality of migration as

> the most natural thing people do, the root of how civilizations, nation-states, and countries were established . . . when white people move . . . it's seen as courageous and necessary, celebrated . . . when people of color move, legally or illegally, the migration itself is subjected

to the question of legality . . . many of us are migrating to countries that previously colonized and imperialized us.[1]

The teleological reliance on the nation-state as a political unit notwithstanding, the allusion to imperial history in *Dear America* never really goes much deeper than an evocative talking point. Still, Vargas points to colonial realities that link diverse histories and migrant communities in ways that I think are remarkably useful. Yet, progressive migrant rights activists would likely consider Vargas's writing part of a more liberal, and less radical, strain of political work on the issue of immigration.[2] Vargas himself points to these critiques simultaneously as gaps in his own work, while also questioning the reasoning behind defining "progressive" politics with such narrow parameters.[3] He disclaims the moniker of "activist," emphasizing that he is not an organizer. He clarifies: "I report, I write, I make documentaries."[4] In short, he is first and foremost a journalist. The perturbed connection and identification as an activist disavowed by more radical corners of immigrant activism is likely due to his, at times, undertheorized commitment to assimilation and Americanization. This manifests in his desire to demonstrate to the country that he has earned his place and thus feels comfortable claiming the category of citizen (as is noted in the title of his autobiography)—a citizen who simply does not have the proper documentation. When filling out employment documentation for a job at the *Chronicle*, he lied about his status by marking a box that affirms his work eligibility, emphasizing: "*But I am going to earn this box.*"[5] Some might say he overcompensates his legal status by centering the American ideals of assimilation and adaptation to liberal capitalism as a productive citizen. There is power in these arguments of expanding the definition of citizenship beyond documentation, and I do not think that their economic rationale should be dismissed out of hand.

It is true that undocumented migrant labor contributes billions of dollars in tax revenue to US society, and those who perform it receive very few of the benefits and entitlements that are awarded to citizens. This perhaps is one of the clearest and purest examples of wage theft. A study by the National Immigration Forum in 2018 discovered that, in 2014, undocumented migrant workers contributed $223.6 billion in federal taxes with little hope of recuperating these funds through access to public systems of support. This amount, when combined with estimated state and local tax contributions, comes to a total of 328.2 billion dollars.[6] Though metrics are markedly different, this amount is comparable to the gross domestic product of the entire nation of the Philippines in 2020, which was approximately $361 billion.[7] In just the state of California, it was concluded that undocumented workers contributed more than *one quarter* of the state's entire tax revenues.[8] In a capitalist society, the recognition of misunderstood and unacknowledged labor can be a powerful antidote to oppression for some, and might lead to opportunities to withhold that labor as a point of political action. This argument presupposes that the recognition of such labor is a vital step toward ending its exploitation. We see this in "Day without immigrants" events that are held in cities across the United States.[9] Events like these are instructive and incredibly important. Nevertheless, mere recognition and visibility of labor, if not taken as a point of departure for more assertive change, may reify capitalism and productivity as the benchmarks for true citizenship. Also, as I will explain further in my analysis, such presumptions may collude with ideologies of ability that presume that the embodiment of the migrant is uniquely capacitated for certain necessary physical labors, while also idealizing an able-body as the most desirable sort of capitalist citizen.[10]

While it is important to point toward perceived limitations in Vargas's worldview and the theoretical and political frameworks that allow us to see them, I am not really interested in leveraging these arguments to dismiss him. His work is powerful, important, approachable, and relatable, and has a place in the immigration landscape of debate toward a more ethical policy and treatment of undocumented people. Yet it is crucial that we contend with the category of the citizen, which not only informs the political impetus and commitment of a spokesman like Vargas, but also provides a structure of thought that emerges in Filipinx and Latinx cultural politics. Citizenship is a vital political structure that merits engagement and expansion; however, it is also true that rendering it the exclusive endpoint and telos of political and critical work has limitations. *Dos X* seeks to excavate these connections in order to critically inhabit the logics of citizenship and, perhaps, delineate alternatives.

Vargas's book offers an important case study that links Filipinx and Latinx studies as fields of thought, experiences, and communities in compelling ways that enrich our understanding of comparative racialization of populations disciplined by the racial exclusions constitutive of citizenship. Vargas is attuned to these ideas better than most and, indeed, for some, he merits exclusion from the immigration rights scene because he is "not even Mexican."[11] This would be a truly damaging exclusion, and constitutes the kind of siloed racial activism that we ought to vigorously militate against. It also speaks to which colonial histories we prioritize as we craft a collective archive on shared dispossession that shapes present-day political activism and policy making on behalf of all. Enacting such myopic exclusion based on racialized essentialism (particularly given the multifarious history of US involvement in the Philippines) reifies past colonial harm, thus reconstituting colonial omission as the standardized racial grammar of political thought and action.[12] Certainly, we would not conceive of a Latinx political agenda or field of study that propagates US colonial intervention in the Philippines by tacitly denying it happened or claiming that it has no bearing on immigration debates in the contemporary moment. While it is true that Vargas has an abiding loyalty to liberalism, his work potentiates thought across Latinx and Filipinx difference that works against the grain of omission, and is thus worthy of our attention and consideration.[13]

I approach his work with a desire to understand someone who upended much of his life self-disclosing his status. Through such publicity, he attained certain privileges, to be sure, but he also put forward good-faith effort to learn more about the forces that innervated his life, and that affected others' lives more deleteriously than his own. I also approach him and his work as a thought-partner, rather than with the predetermined goal to advance prescriptivist statements on what progressive politics ought to be. I am more interested in why he makes the choices he does and what the socio-political forces were that shape subjectivity and constrain agency in articulating those choices. I am particularly interested in the ways in which we can map such constraints through the politics and optics of racial misrecognition. With an eye toward the genre of autobiography, I approach my critique with the knowledge that the politics of reading, self-disclosure, and self-authorship are complex. I also consider his text from the perspective of someone who, for a time, had an unstable resident status in the United States; I thus feel personally hailed by the community whose stories Vargas attempts to tell as part of the work of his non-profit media organization "Define American"—an organization whose work he models after and aligns with GLAAD (Gay and Lesbian Alliance Against Defamation). Such affective bonds are brought about by substantiated childhood fears of the real possibility of deportation and the generalized anxiety or paranoia surfaced by ambiguous legal status. These are anxieties that I have felt personally and that, to my mind, constitute an important epistemology. Such negative affect pervades many migrant communities across the world and across time.

In order to get at comparative racial connections between Latinx and Filipinx cultural politics, I am drawn to the ways that Vargas makes sense of the (racial) politics of passing and misrecognition. In an interview with Vargas published in Columbia University's *Journal of International Affairs*, the first question posed to him prominently exposes the conundrum that I highlight in this chapter:

> In other interviews, you have discussed the fact that people have often assumed you are Mexican because your name is Jose. What reflections do you have on this? Do you often feel as though people are often surprised that you are undocumented and from the Philippines?[14]

Vargas responds with a critique that US mainstream political discourse has greatly narrowed the immigration debate's racial terms, conflating illegality with Mexicanness (and perhaps Central America). He appeals to the history of the US as a nation of immigrants—one that ought to critically include "the circle of Asian and Latino immigrants in this country."[15] In his memoir, this surfaces via the ways that Filipinx subjectivity as undocumented or migrant is embedded in modes of racial address that inevitably cite Latinx identities.[16] His engagement with the politics of "passing" threads these multiple modes of address together. However, he mostly uses "Passing" (the title of the second section of his memoir) as a framework to understand his legal status; i.e., he passed as a bona fide legal citizen or resident of the United States. Nevertheless, passing takes on meaning vis-à-vis his ethnonational identity as a Filipino, and his disclosure as undocumented within an immigration debate whose landscape is perhaps overdetermined by the US-Mexico border. In that sense, Vargas's disclosure diversifies the population about which we are speaking when we reference and make claims on and as the immigrant. Thus, passing is also ineluctably and recursively wedded to misrecognition and resistance to being recognized as Latino or, more specifically in *Dear America*, Mexican. He references with some regularity that the master narrative that he wants to disabuse his readers of is that Mexicans are exclusively the undocumented, DACA recipients are only those of Latin American descent, and that the physical border is the principal geography that grounds immigrant politics. Vargas, when detained in Texas in 2014, affirms defiantly to a Latino border control officer that "[his] border was the Pacific Ocean."[17] However, given the ways that Vargas measures his own agency through a citizenship that he has and must earn through capitalist productivity, robust intellectual contributions to US society through award-winning journalism, and wealthy, white support networks that helped ensure his safety, a problematic racial affect emerges in his rhetoric that merits our attention and engagement. I describe this as an affect of "undocumentality."

Undocumentality is a form of racial sentimentality that produces a sympathetic immigrant subject worthy of rescue. Succinctly, I define undocumentality as a liberal affect producing sentimental attachment to the undocumented. It is directed toward a white readership in order to circumvent the fear of and anxiety around malingering. That is, representations of undocumentality construct a migrant subject that is shown to be industrious, high-achieving, and advantageous to the society in which they live, thus facilitating a sympathetic attachment that circumvents the charge of indolence, truancy, and larceny often accompanying "illegality." In many ways, this affect aligns with model minority stereotypes of the Asian American success story.[18] Instead, undocumentality rightly points out the exploitative labor dynamics that are at play, and that constitute the engine of racial capitalism. In the aforementioned interview, Vargas observes about Los Angeles that "[the city] would collapse without Mexican labor."[19] Nevertheless, I suggest that such ideas, while well-intentioned, tend to capitulate to ableist capitalist demands for productivity and reify value extraction as the rationality of the citizen. While it points out exploitation in the near term, it also rhetorically solidifies its conditions of possibility. Nevertheless, this paradox speaks not to moral judgments we should make about undocumented people that decide to inhabit their status in this way. Rather, it speaks more compellingly to the field of constrained agency that limits the horizon of choices that are left to many undocumented people who cannot afford the luxury of radicality enjoyed by academic critics and activists who experience the comfort of the citizenship that they critique. What I state here is not a very new argument in many ways. Many scholars in the fields of ethnic studies and Asian American studies have pointed out the historical contradiction of the ostensive universalism of the franchise of citizenship, while empirically demonstrating that it has relied extensively—constitutively—on racialized, immigrant, foreign, and alien non-citizen labor as a mechanism of wealth generation.[20] Vargas points stridently to this contradiction that mirrors the academic arguments on similar phenomena. He writes: "Immigrants are seen as mere labor, our physical bodies judged by perceptions of what we contribute, or what we take. Our existence is as broadly criminalized as it is commodified."[21]

Migrant alien labor generates wealth for the citizen, while perpetually being categorically excluded from citizenship. This also reduces the migrant to mere embodiment. My reading has disability implications, in that the very existence of the unfettered citizen has historically relied on embodied, yet abstracted, migrant labor to nourish citizenship itself as a liberal democratic ideal. This ideal is constituted through notions of independence, self-determination, and individuality. Vargas shows that this unfettered independence is a racial fantasy. Following Julie Avril Minich's arguments on the matter, this dynamic demonstrates the ways that the able-bodied citizen, in order to ensure his independence, prothet-icizes the alien non-citizen to buoy citizenship as an ableist institution.[22] Significantly, this liberal construction of the citizen as racially white, productive, and able-bodied has materialized through imperial expansion and integration of foreign territories—histories that are particularly salient and that are, at least partly, the underlying mode of production for Vargas's Filipinx memoir. Conservative and centrist arguments that we are a "nation of laws" with clearly defined borders can only hold water if they omit these histories in which US foreign policy was predicated on violating precisely these principles that uphold the citizen.[23] We might think of alternative definitions of the citizen that are reparative and that redress these histories of empire.

Despite this historical context, Vargas's memoir does not quite move in these historical waters consistently. Interestingly, he gives more attention to the histories of the US-Mexico Borderlands, the treaty of Guadalupe-Hidalgo (1848), and the US acquisition of formerly Mexican territories.[24] This demonstrates the extent to which Mexican American histories and racial identity more prominently shape even this Filipinx narrative of self-disclosure and the immigration debate more broadly. The intercalation and mutual superimposition of these histories demonstrate that *Dear America* serves as a cultural and historical crossroads. I wish to explore this crossroads, which manifests in a couple of ways. First, it definitively shows the ways that Latinx diasporas are the fundamental racial discourse through which we apprehend immigration policy and reform. This is far from arbitrary and is, indeed, sometimes politically necessary, given the ways in which they are perennially cited by Vargas himself. However, I aver to demonstrate how this unavoidable Latinx citation is imbricated with Filipinx subjectivity and embodiment. Thus, the second point I illuminate is the ways in which Vargas surfaces this cross-racial encounter through an adaptive politics of resistance to misrecognition. This is understandable, in that naturally we wish to be recognized for who we are, rather than being interchangeable with distinct migrants. I suggest, however, that these moments of racial misrecognition as Latinx are ambivalently resisted and provide a productive opportunity to understand the nature of cultural and racial interposition. What might racial error be productive of? What is the methodological and theoretical frame of reference through which to understand a Filipino American being constantly misrecognized as Latino, Mexican, or Central American? Latinx studies? Filipinx American studies? Or a combination of both? The fact that a text like this exists, detailing a multivalent experience such as Vargas's, suggests that comparative racial politics and ethnic studies have a pivotal role in shaping the immigration debate—particularly as it pertains to expressive culture and self-authorship.

In what follows, I offer analysis of these moments of crossroads that are charted in Vargas's disclosure of his legal status as undocumented. I argue that these instances, taken together, offer rich insights on the ways in which we can utilize cultural production and politics to map the coordinates of a more unified Latinx and Filipinx studies whose connections are partly articulated through subtended, yet shared, histories of colonial encounter. These colonialisms are those of Spain and the United States, whose intersecting realities in many of the nations of the world are also bound profoundly together in the diasporic populations of the Philippines and Latin America in the United States. This interconnection demonstrates that comparative ethnic studies must attend closely to comparative empire. Additionally, it shows that the constellating work of the dos x of Latinx and Filipinx studies potentiates these fields as an anti-imperial co-formation that captures an understanding of the politics of race within a truly global matrix.

## Misrecognition in the Brown Commons

*Dear America* prominently and provocatively titles one of its chapters "Mexican José and Filipino Jose."[25] The juxtaposition of the name "José" with "Jose" does aesthetic work in pointing to a distinction that Vargas foregrounds, and to which he recursively returns throughout his memoir. In ways that strikingly mirror the politics of "correct" Spanish usage that are surfaced by the x in Latinx or Filipinx, the absence of an accent furnishes a non-Spanish Jose—a not grammatically precise Jose. Indeed, the potential to eviscerate binary gender regimes through an insistence on the x could also, perhaps, be productively read as a disloyalty to the geopolitical and racial stability enshrined in Latinx. If Latinx is a queer, antisocial posture that accommodates and critically centers gender non-conforming subjects marginalized by ethnonational patriarchy, then might the x be extended to subjects that might structurally be non-compliant racially? This is a roundabout way of hailing Filipinx Americans as aligned with the antisocial political maneuvers of Latinx, which questions our allegiance to binary gender constructs.[26] Do, indeed, the attempts to lessen the burdens of gender dysphoria through the substantiation of more inclusive political communities map in similar ways onto the experience of racial dysphoria, which manifests as a symptom and product of racial misrecognition?

Such questioning, I suggest, fits into recurring observations in *Dear America* that "Filipinos fit everywhere and nowhere at all."[27] During his coming of age as a somewhat new immigrant to the United States growing up in California, Vargas "wasn't sure how a Filipino was supposed to look, or where a Filipino was supposed to fit."[28] The paradoxical observation that Filipinos were invisible, yet also universally present, resonates with the realities of Filipino labor migration—a reality that Vargas mentions, and that has been extensively studied.[29]

It is important to note that the scene in which he formally meets the bureaucratic apparatus of the US nation-state (the California Department of Motor Vehicles) is not only shaped by the belated discovery of the lie engineered by his grandfather and mother, but also evokes the anxiety of racial misrecognition. After handing the DMV worker his permanent resident card and school ID,

> she examined the green card, flipping it around, twice. Furrowing her brows, she then lowered her head, leaned over, and whispered, "This is fake. Don't come back here again."
>
> Fake.
>
> Instantly, I thought she was mistaken, perhaps even lying. She seemed surprised that I didn't know that the green card was fake . . .
>
> *Of course she's lying.*
>
> *How can it be fake?*
>
> As I approached Mi Pueblo, a Mexican market where Lola and I sometimes shopped for mangoes and rice, my heart stopped.
>
> *Maybe the woman at the DMV thought I was Mexican? Because, you know, my name is Jose even though it's not José?*[30]

Note the ways that Vargas's Filipino embodiment is in dialectical tension with the space of California, conceived prominently as a space in the US-Mexico Borderlands. The assertion of selfhood as legitimate and legal is thus implicitly aligned with being Filipino, a sense produced through a disidentification with Mi Pueblo. Presumed Mexican illegality risks contaminating Filipinoness. And yet, he marks a sense of conviviality with Mexicans in that he and his grandmother shop at Mi Pueblo "for mangoes and rice." Filipino identity, its relationship with the state, and citizenship are in co-formal exchange with the US-Mexico Borderlands and Mexican identity. While Vargas earlier states that he "wasn't sure how a Filipino was supposed to look," his impressions of the ways that the DMV worker misidentified him implicitly cite a common racialized brownness that Vargas attempts to navigate through remonstrances rooted in his Filipino difference—he is "Filipino Jose" not "Mexican José." This is a complaint that resurfaces later in his narrative. Such interpellations indicate that Vargas's Filipino brownness is in recursive definition embedded in the Borderlands space of California, which, as established by authors like Gloria Anzaldúa, María Josefina Saldaña-Portillo, and others, is a space that is already in historical and racial flux.[31] As an immigrant youth coming to self-knowledge in a "migrant imaginary" shaped by anti-Mexican animus, Filipinx ontology seems partially scripted by an avowed distance from Mexican criminality and a racist bureaucratic gaze that might tend to render Filipinos interchangeable with Mexicans.[32] It seems that Vargas lets it slip that the state may have gotten it right were he actually Mexican. Filipinos, as implicitly articulated in Vargas's narration of his belated discovery of illegality, are preferably understood as legally compliant to immigration law, while Mexicans are not. Although these are certainly contrary to views Vargas will share later, his narrative here seems to retrench Mexicans as the object of illegality from which Filipinos ought to disidentify. The linkage of Mexicanness to criminality is why the risk of misrecognition is so concerning to him.

Even so, despite the distinction that Vargas is affecting here, there is a potent allusion to similitude—the ironic decoupling of the name Jose: "my name is Jose though it's not José." This produces an uncanny rhetorical effect that surreptitiously surfaces a shared colonial encounter under Spanish colonialism—that is why a Filipino and a Mexican can both be named "José." This is also why a Filipino can find himself passing a grocery called Mi Pueblo in territory that used to be part of Mexico. However, this affinity is circumvented and replaced by the racial differentiations that are meaningful under US immigration law. The anxiety over racial substitution, interchangeability, and error ("all brown people look alike") is productive of a set of emotional responses and attachments that shape the experience of diasporic subjectivity anchored in a common brownness.

José Esteban Muñoz argued for a different kind of disidentification not rooted in the precise sorting of migrants into batchable people categorized via a racial heuristic that colludes with state power assumed to be the arbiter of defining the good from bad migrants. As Joshua Takano Chambers-Letson and Tavia Amolo Ochieng' Nyongó write in their foreword to the posthumous *The Sense of Brown*, Muñoz theorizes disidentification not through distinction, but through a "strategic obliquity" that eschews essentialism and "transparent address to identity."[33] Instead, identification materializes through and "[resonates] within a 'structure of feeling' that cuts through certain Latino and queer communities."[34] My own brown sense is that the strategic obliquity to which Muñoz spoke can laterally and horizontally cut across communities rather than merely or exclusively within them. Vargas provides a roadmap, in a manner of speaking, which paradoxically emerges through an exploration of his anxiety to *not* identify with or as Mexican due to the fear of illegality. What sorts of coalitional, affective, and political bonds can emerge through racial relations that are governed by an incessant desire to collapse racialized migrants under the universalist rubric of "illegal," on the one hand, and yet also evokes discursive processes that anchor the "illegal" to Mexican embodiment and subjectivity, on the other? Here I mean a mode of reading the misrecognition and anxiety about it within an economy of racial meanings that avoids easy recourse into discrete unimpeachable difference. Rather than assume, however implicitly or unconsciously, that Mexican identification is the bad object one must cast into social death while US citizenship is the good object with which we ought to identify, I suggest we explore what is revealed in the very observation of this racial slippage that seems to structure the integration of Filipinos into the nation by passing them through a prism of Mexicanness.[35]

Muñoz argued that unlike queerness, which is on a horizon of possibility that is perpetually deferred, brownness is an immanent reality that is already here. The certitude with which Muñoz identified brownness contrasts with the antisocial subjectlessness of queerness. Queer scholars have understood queer identity and theory as an antisocial political posture that materializes a critique of normativity, rather than a sociological or empirical definition of sexual identity.[36] What this means in practice is that there ought not to be one identity around which we organize queer identity or critique. It is open to interpretation and resignification, and is mutable. For this reason, queerness is an ideality that will never quite concretize—that is its political power. Brownness, by contrast, is rooted in "everyday styles of loving that connote illegitimacy."[37] It is a quotidian rather than idealized "anti-identitarian concept" that materializes solidarity through a sameness that reads against the grain of "Hispanic" and hails " 'brown' as in brown people in an immediate way . . . people who are rendered brown by their personal and familial participations in North to South migration patterns."[38] So, while it, like queerness, possesses antisocial political qualities that contest the material conditions of oppression, it is defined through material, historically grounded, and empirical realities of migration, and a shared identification around those realities. Queerness, by comparison, facilitates a subjectless position that ideally resemanticizes the ground upon which queer politics is grounded—Judith Butler calls this the "ungrounded ground" upon which queerness is articulated.[39] While Muñoz's visioning of brownness can facilitate similar adaptive course corrections that dislodge political subjects as the exclusive center around which political claims are staked, the new subject for whom that center is dislodged likely shares the "quotidian illegitimacy" materially grounded in a shared reality of migration, labor exploitation, and familial kinship. These grounded realities are delineated in concert with ethnonational identifications that queerness does *not* share. There is no queer nation-state from which émigrés depart to participate in the vicissitudes of racial capitalism, to then embrace a new assimilated national identity that demands conformity. Queerness can certainly intersect with such realities, but does not materially define them in the same ways.[40]

Vargas's memoir recapitulates some of these ideas around a brown commons that summons a community into existence. Indeed, the queer "sense of brown" illuminates the queerness of interrace in ways that Vargas's own gay identity does not. From the perspective of a queer Filipinx reader, Vargas's homosexuality is not an overwhelmingly central feature of his memoir—he often evades representing intimacy or sex in his life narrative. The moving reasoning he shares for why this evasion exists ("Romantic entanglements are out of the question") is paradoxically related to how open he could be as a gay man. Because he was in the closet about his legal status, he desired and reveled in the freedom of being out of the closet. Gayness offered a sense of authenticity and openness that he lacked. His queerness was a refuge, as he was able to step into that space of identity disclosure that was not possible as a bona fide citizen otherwise.[41] Moreover, gay political activism and visibility politics shape his own work in Define American, which, as I have mentioned, Vargas based on GLAAD: "taking a page from the playbook of the LGBTQ rights movement, we believe that you cannot change the politics of immigration until you change the culture in which immigrants are seen."[42] For him this involves storytelling—humanizing the abstraction that is the undocumented, and thus mobilizing an affective sympathy that is required for such a task. Nevertheless, the perceptual lack of engagement with queerness, at least compared with his reckonings with race, is also precisely about the transience he feels as an undocumented migrant. The psychic transience he feels due to the ambiguity of his status translates into the impossibility of attachment. Such transience might point to the ways that queer sexuality can only be properly experienced as a robust feature of liberal rights-based personhood within the enabling structures of citizenship and the permanence that it provides. Perhaps alien "illegal" non-citizens have many other reasons for why their sexualities are contra national norms irreducible to same-sex desire. Furthermore, queerness, it seems, was not something that had to be "earned"—this might explain why one coming-out was easier than the other for Vargas. Significantly though, homophobia structures his thinking on immigrant equality. He refused a female friend's proposal to secure citizenship through marriage, arguing that such a right should be available to gay immigrants. This significantly establishes Vargas as not capitulating to the malingering stereotypes that circulate about illegals who would presumably use fake marriages to acquire citizenship (this also assumes that "real" marriages are any less transactional, but that is a topic for another paper). Despite these important observations, the queerness of sexuality is quite secondary to the queerness of race in *Dear America*. What I mean by racial queerness is the instability of identification to which I have been referring throughout, wherein Filipinx identity is situated at an unstable multiracial crossroads.

## On Racial Dysphoria and Black Madness

The misrecognitions that substantively structure parts of Vargas's narrative are born from overlapping realities of migration, labor politics, and shared histories of colonial encounter. Even so, the sense that is made out of these misrecognitions does capitulate to some of the damaging ideas around exclusionary citizenship propelled by anti-Mexican animus, even while materializing a productive critique rooted in a common brownness. I suggest that misrecognition constitutes a structure of feeling that inhibits both upward social mobility and ascendant or aspirational whiteness. It constitutes a blockage—an "ugly feeling," to use Sianne Ngai's term—that paradoxically represents an opportunity to question the very logic of assimilation and development itself.[43] There is a "diagnostic" quality that surfaces in the inhibited ability of Filipinos to be recognized as themselves and who are instead collapsed into Mexican identity. The ugly feeling of misrecognition (the rejection of the social death of illegality) evokes a constrained agency of inhabiting or being inhabited by error, and thus is indicative of a type of racial dysphoria that occasions moments of productive maladjustment with colonial citizenship.[44] Ngai has forcefully analyzed non-cathartic affects that are not anchored in specific objects, and are instead generalized and indeterminate. Affects like paranoia, anxiety, or irritation (unlike fear, anger, or jealousy) oscillate between the internal subjective feeling and the lack of a discernible external reality grounded in a specific object that produces the feeling, or upon which the feeling is directed. For instance, one is afraid of something—an actual object that produces fear. Meanwhile, anxiety may be triggered, unbeknownst to the subject, by a stimulus that is more atmospheric and diffuse. For Ngai, this indeterminacy is actually productive, as it offers the opportunity to diagnose a complex and diffuse set of social relations that are not overdetermined by a "philic striving" toward material objects as the basis of critique. Instead, meaning can be made from the "trajectories of repulsion" and the conditions which shape our "phobic strivings 'away from'" the indeterminacy of dysphoria.[45] What this means for an analysis of a Filipinx inhabiting or being identified through "Latinidad" is centering racial error and misrecognition, rather than phobically receding and fetishizing correction.

This brings me to the affect of undocumentation in Vargas's memoir. This affect is characterized by a national phobic repulsion away from the undocumented. In response to this national repellant feeling, Vargas leverages an affect of undocumentality that engineers a sympathetic migrant subject whose own sense of indeterminacy renders equally indeterminate the negativity that is typically derogatively invested in undocumented people—a population that is often considered the refuse of the citizen and the underside of citizenship itself. Nevertheless, Filipinx undocumentality's own indeterminacy is irrevocably situated in the indeterminate racial misrecognitions that compromise stable Filipinx American identification as a discrete category of migrant experience. As I have established above, Vargas's work or appearance as a Filipinx undocumented migrant is typically belated. That is, it is deferred by the necessary initial navigation through Mexican (mis)identification. The sympathy elicited by the genre of assimilation, social mobility, and professional respectability commanded by Vargas is accompanied by a double of the Mexican; at the same time, however, Filipinx identity is enmeshed with Mexicanness in an immigration landscape that is overdetermined (not arbitrarily so) by the US-Mexico border. Like the ugly feelings that Ngai examines, whose own indeterminacy is tantamount to a "suspended agency" for the feeler that feels them, might Filipinx racial identity itself constitute an agency suspended by the logic of perennial misrecognitions? Misrecognition that is the product of a multiracial imaginary of liberal citizenship conditioned by the philic attachment to the United States as a nation of immigrants?

How might we reckon with a diasporic migrant personhood that is complexly latticed with the subjectivity of another with whom one shares racialized physical characteristics, interchangeable under processes of racialized capital, but from whom one is empirically distinct at the same time? My argument here is that this racial uncanny potentially registers an agency and intention toward the other that are paradoxically anchored to the epistemological uncertainty produced through misrecognition. Uncanniness inevitably circulates in Vargas's autobiography, I contend, through its thematic engagement with the politics of passing to which I have already alluded. I have observed that passing for Vargas is much more in dialogue with migrant legal status; however, it also circulates within an economy of racial identifiers that quilt across Latinx and Filipinx racial sameness and distinction. Vargas advances a moving and insightful argument that passing is not an independent venture. Rather, it is embedded in networks of support—a migrant does not pass unless there is an informal structure of care that facilitates that passing. The implication might be that no single migrant breaks the law, but the law is bent, distended, and fragmented by a community of passersby, who note and advance the act of passing. Given the diffuse nature of passing, it makes little sense to label individuals or discrete communities as illegal; passing is a "crime" that is committed across vast networks, where the abstractions of law do not venture. Vargas beautifully remarks that

> There is no passing alone.
>
> At every challenging, complicated, and complicating juncture of my life—getting to college, getting a job, getting a driver's license so I could have valid proof of identification so I could get a job, keeping a job—a stranger who did not remain a stranger saved me . . .
>
> I know for sure that all these Americans—all these strangers, all across the country—have allowed people like me to pass.
>
> If just five people—a friend, a co-worker, a classmate, a neighbor, a faith leader—helped out one of the estimated 11 million undocumented people in our country, then illegal immigration as we know [it] would touch at least 66 million people.[46]

This passage appears in a chapter entitled "Strangers." It evokes what historian Nayan Shah has called "stranger intimacies" that can "produce egalitarian social and political arenas, ethics, and associations."[47] It is important to note that the strangers to which Vargas expresses gratitude are, by his own admission, wealthy professional networks of "White People" (also the title of a chapter in his autobiography). This is significant, as these interactions are much less tense than those he has with other people of color. For instance, (while this is a small detail, it is suggestive) he first discloses his status to his professional mentor Peter Perl, who was the director of the newsroom at the *Washington Post* when Vargas worked there. They met when Vargas worked at the *Post* as a summer intern. In this conversation, Vargas finds understanding, comfort, and friendship. This contrasts with his interaction with another mentor, Lynne Duke, who also worked at the *Post* and took Vargas "under her wing."[48] She was one of several Black women working at the newspaper, according to Vargas. He reports that when the opportunity presented itself to "tell Lynne what was eating me up," he "stopped himself." He reflects that he "wasn't prepared for whatever her reaction would be."[49] It is suggestive to me that Duke is not included in the stranger intimacy support network that he beautifully renders just a few pages prior to this moment. Passing, for Vargas, articulates a subterranean horizontal comradeship—to borrow a turn-of-phrase from Benedict Anderson—unbeknownst to most Americans, who might participate with acts of kindness and mentorship in ethical encounters with the undocumented.[50] Because passing is a communal (perhaps national) activity, it fits within Vargas's efforts to inflect his experience with a rhetorical mode of moral suasion that concretizes the undocumented as thinking-feeling humans, rather than abstracting them.

Nevertheless, it seems that implicitly Duke, the Black woman for whom he was a protégé and whose mentorship he "cherished," is not quite a part of the stranger network of facilitated-passing that substantiates the clandestine integration of undocumented people across the United States. Interestingly, Vargas comments that, with other Black women journalists, Duke "formed a kind of sisterhood: they championed one another, and, for some reason, they all ended up guiding me in some way."[51] This is not the only time that Black professionals constitute a source of succor and mentorship for Vargas. Several times throughout *Dear America*, Vargas liberally draws on Black thought to make deeper meaning out of his experience as undocumented. At one point in his narrative, he observes that he "hung up posters of Toni Morrison, James Baldwin, and Maya

Angelou, who comprise what [he] considers [his] holy trinity of spiritual guidance."[52]

In a particularly noteworthy passage earlier in his autobiography, Vargas comments on the ways that he, as a young man learning about US race relations, wrestled with the ways that a Black-white binary seemed to structure the idea of race in American society. Again, drawing on Black thought and art, he reflects:

> I didn't realize it as such, but I was struggling to understand the construction of that binary, trying to unlock why "white" and "black" became an obsession for me, which was fueled even more when I first read Toni Morrison's *The Bluest Eye*.[53]

It is worth noting that this citation of Morrison is followed by a quick timeline charting a history of the relationship between race and immigration with the arrival of Anglo settlers ("the first peoples who populated this land, Native Americans, were not considered United States citizens until 1924"), the Chinese Exclusion Act of 1882 ("not repealed until 1943"), and the Naturalization Act of 1790, which Vargas notes was "the country's first set of laws dealing with citizenship," indicating that only free white people could be considered citizens. Vargas's subjectivity as an undocumented person and his race consciousness in the United States confronted the stark histories of settler colonialism, anti-Chinese racism, and antiblackness. This draws a line from his critique of racial capitalism's distillation of aliens into mere embodiment to the history of chattel slavery's reduction of personhood into property, and thus to philosophical negation of their rights to citizenship.

The historical crossroads that misrecognition furnishes is contextualized within a racial framework that is crucial for understanding the American racial landscape. Vargas relies on a "trinity" of Black thinkers and cultural producers as his moral guide. This, for some reason, does not provoke a need to delineate a clear border between Black and Filipinx, for instance. Rather than drawing upon Filipino philosophers, artists, or scholars, or perhaps Mexican/Latinx ones, Vargas's ethical compasses are Black thought and art. These form the basis of the ways that he conceives of American race relations. The affective dimension that this "trinity" takes in *Dear America* is one of admiration, awe, and philosophical gravity. It does not foment a need to articulate a distinct identitarian border, as he does with Mexicans. This is because he is able to position the "immigrant" as distinct from "Native Americans" and "African Americans," whose relationship to migration is, of course, constitutively different.[54] Nevertheless, such histories of Indigenous and Black dispossession signal racialized populations whose own relationship with citizenship is vexed, and thus generates crucial affinities that are significant for Vargas's observations. While these affinities extend to Black philosophical, aesthetic, and political representations of race, they do not quite translate to inviting the Black people in Vargas's life to participate in his own networks of passing that he elaborates. Nevertheless, such ideas align in their ability to explain the subjective and psychological experience of racism as it is articulated in the master narrative of illegality. He identifies significantly with Morrison's Pecola in her novel *The Bluest Eye*. Pecola's experience of madness becomes a lens through which the psycho-affective contours of undocumentality obtain.

As a young man, presumably before even reaching his twenties, Vargas "ran across a replay of an interview . . . between Morrison and the journalist Bill Moyers" on a PBS program called "A World of Ideas." Vargas reproduces a portion of the transcript of the interview in his memoir, worth quoting at length, as it provides a definitive idea of how Vargas was able to recognize the racialized existence of being undocumented via Morrison's narrative rendering of the psychological experience of oppression and racism:

> Moyers: I don't think I've ever met a more pathetic creature in contemporary literature than Pecola Breedlove . . . .
>
> Abused by her—
>
> Morrison: Everybody.
>
> Moyers: —parents, rejected by her neighbors, ugly, homely, alone. Finally *descending into madness* . . . It's been years since I read that novel, but I remember her.
>
> Morrison: She surrendered completely to the so-called master narrative.
>
> Moyers: To?
>
> Morrison: The master narrative, I mean, the whole notion of what is ugliness, what is worthlessness, what is contempt. She got it from her family, she got it from school, she got it from the movies, she got it everywhere.
>
> Moyers: The master narrative. What is—that's life?
>
> Morrison: No, it's white male life. The master narrative is whatever ideological script that is being imposed on everybody else. The master

> fiction. History. It has a certain point of view. So, when these little girls see that the most prized gift that they can get at Christmastime is this little white doll, that's the master narrative speaking. "This is beautiful, this is lovely, and you're not it." . . . She is so needful, so completely needful, has so little, needs so much, she becomes the perfect victim.[55]

*The Bluest Eye* is particularly noteworthy as it details a Black girl who desires whiteness. She is forced to comply with a white ideal of beauty and self-worth that engulfs any kind of authentic subjectivity she may have developed without racist violence. Vargas relates this to the lie of his legal status—a web of deception that he wishes to extricate himself from. Pecola becomes a touchstone for him:

> I would come back to Pecola's story again and again, unlocking whatever meaning I could find . . . Pecola was a year younger than I was when I came to the U.S. [and] our lives couldn't have been any more different, save for one central detail: we were both lied to.[56]

For Vargas, self-disclosure and coming out become aspects of a cathartic resolution of violent self-perception—an exit out of the "perfect victimhood" explored by Morrison. Nevertheless, these dimensions of expression are powerfully bound up with Pecola's cognition.

A crucial observation in the Moyers-Morrison exchange is Pecola's "descent" into madness. This madness constitutes the "pathetic" state of victimhood from which Vargas wants to escape. Thus, while there is an identification with the critical contribution of Black thought in making sense of American race relations, there is a fear of insanity that circumscribes one's journey to conquer the big lie of racism. "Black madness" seems operative here in demonstrating the toxic consequences of believing the lie—the master narrative or master fiction of "white male life."[57] Even Morrison responds to Moyers's diagnosis of Pecola by indicating a surrender to the ideological compromise of racism—Pecola's madness becomes the evidence of the ways that racism and white supremacy can really hurt people—young Black girls in particular. Vargas's identification of Morrison's critical take on racist ideology extends to a disidentification with the madness that encircles Pecola's psyche. He indeed discloses in his narrative that he was depressed.[58] Additionally, in relation to his self-diagnosis of depression, he comments on the psychic burden unduly placed on him by needing to live two lives, his constant fear of being found out, and the distress of potentially being deported back to the Philippines, when he considers the United States his true home. Throughout his autobiography, he publicizes his undocumented distress occasioned by his legal ambiguity in ways that render depression "a cultural and social phenomenon rather than a medical disease."[59] This meshes well with his argument that passing is a social process embedded in diverse networks of support. Vargas's engagement with madness, depression, and affective distress more explicitly links the ways disability shapes the contours of the undocumentality that frames his autobiography. The sympathetic migrant's plight and affective dysphoria, dyadically articulated between alien malingerer and upstanding citizen-subject, signal the debilitated state of existence that exclusion from capacitated citizenship produces. The fact that this illegality is explained through an engagement with Morrison's representation of Pecola as mad is telling. This suggests that the proper citizen is a not-mad one. If undocumentality, as I have been describing it, is the affective representation of a sympathetic migrant subject worthy of American citizenship, this sympathy is generated partly from the migrant desire to not be mad like Pecola.

I introduce this momentous engagement with Morrison to highlight the ways that the racial disjunctive feeling of misrecognition is elaborated in a continuum with representations of Black disenfranchisement. This is so because of the ways that Black cultural politics frame Vargas's understanding of race as a new(er) immigrant to the United States. The engagement with Black thought takes on significantly more discursive real estate, given how Vargas distances himself from, say, Latinx, Chicanx, or Mexican American cultural identity, and given the ways that, in his experience, these have engulfed and ethnographically entrapped his own specificity as Filipino.[60] I have been arguing throughout this chapter that this affect of racial disjuncture, this dysphoria, and its subsequent genesis in and generation of racial misrecognition are all rooted in a recognition of a mutually shared station of racial disposability under racial capitalism. The anxiety around being racially atomistic and interchangeable subjects reflects a slippage that indexes one's relationship to the modes of capitalist production. Vargas bemoans the reduction of the immigrant to mere embodiment, implicating a critique of the ableist ideologies undergirding citizenship. In the realm of self-representation, cultural production evokes desire for the vaunted subject position of the liberal citizen-subject as productive, sane, and able-bodied. My hope is to think through the ways that Filipinx-Latinx misrecognition indexes this mutually encompassing social location under the inaccessible auspices of US citizenship and, I suggest, potentiates alternatives to the politics of disposability. These alternatives find ground through a refinement of the affinities that are paradoxically assigned through erroneous recognitions. I note that it is of significance that the elaboration of racial disjunctive feeling (and its amelioration through a rhetorical tactic of undocumentality) finds ground via the connection of interracial disposability with a foundational Black negativity. Black disenfranchisement and oppression become a heuristic filter allowing Vargas to gain analytical purchase on the meanings of American racialization. As I have elaborated, this is exemplified by the extensive citation of Morrison and her diagnosis of the faults of US race relations. Notably, madness anchors this engagement. The diasporic subjectivity of which Vargas is a part dialogues with what La Marr Jurelle Bruce has productively imagined as "mad diasporas."[61]

Linking Michel Foucault's fictive "ship of fools" with the transatlantic slave ship, Bruce defines "mad diaspora" as the dispersal of bodies populating a "fruitless expanse of two countries that cannot belong" to them. He clarifies this as "a scattering of captives across sovereign borders and over bodies of water; an upheaval and dispersal of persons flung far from home; and an emergence of unprecedented diasporic subjectivities, ontologies, and possibilities that transgress national and rational norms."[62] In order to support his project of articulating a "radical black creativity," he foregrounds a desire to suspend empiricism and the fetish of rationality premised on the truly mad institution of slavery and psychiatric carcerality that condition the modern and its enlightened principles of empirical truth. Significantly, these enlightened ideologies are the very substance of the institution of citizenship that is of central concern both to undocumented diasporic subjectivity and to the institution from which "captives" (the institutionalized and the enslaved) are in a state of suspended limbo between "two countries," "dispersed," scattered "across sovereign borders." This mimics the experience and condition of suspended agency occasioned by undocumentedness—a limbo, a "nowhere at all," whose psychic cost produces a wounded migrant subject that identifies with the psychic victimhood of "Black madness," to again borrow language from Therí Alyce Pickens. Thinking through Pickens's "Black madness," Cvetkovich's social phenomenology of depression, and Bruce's stirring advancement of a "mad methodology" that recuperates subrational epistemologies and the social (rather than biomedical) analysis of normally private conditions, all align significantly with the affective parameters of Vargas's undocumentality. This is functionalized in the genre of autobiography—which is a genre that, by definition, renders the interior private life of the subject a public work.

The move from private interiority of the abstract undocumented subject to public problem in control of his own narrative converges with ethnic studies critiques of racial capital, insofar as it centers the realm of the beleaguered affects of an undocumented citizenry as an exploited class of laborers. This is so because both disability studies and ethnic studies critiques of racial capitalism resist measuring self-worth through productivity. They also do not capitulate to logics restoring the self to optimal labor capacity in order to contribute advantage to the citizen (thus "earning" their citizenship in the process). Black madness as the subrational underside to the rational US citizen is the substratum upon which, by Vargas's own admission, Filipinx undocumented subjectivity is articulated autobiographically. The coordinates of undocumentedness are scoped not only within the "afterlife of slavery," but also in spaces of carcerality (which themselves are extensions of this history).[63] Carceral space in the Borderlands concludes Vargas's memoir with perhaps the most stunning misrecognition yet.

## Mexican Names

In a processing interview with a Mexican American border agent, Vargas is asked "Did you cross the border?" To which he responds, "No. My border was the Pacific Ocean." Allaying the recurrent confusion of the agent as to Vargas's providence, he affirms, perhaps defiantly, "I'm from the Philippines." The agent who works as part of border security for the "benefits" (as Vargas calls them) remarks: "Hey, I know someone from the Philippines. You guys have Mexican names." Vargas sees him place an accent on his "Mexican name," which he promptly corrects: "I stopped him and said that Filipinos, for reasons I don't fully understand, don't put accents on our Spanish names . . . it's our way of rebelling against Spanish colonialism. Or something like that."[64] For his name that is decidedly Spanish, by his own admission, he exerts a level of agentive defiance through that same name that has been wrongly interpellated as Mexican: "I might not be able to control what was happening, but I was going to control the punctuation of my name . . . My name is Jose because of Spanish colonialism. But Jose isn't José because of American imperialism. Even my name isn't really mine."[65] Vargas is uncanny to himself, inhabiting multiple modes of address that fracture his subjectivity. He is dispossessed from his self via a name that is oddly foreign to him—it fits wrong, yet is undoubtedly *his*, as evinced by his efforts to protect its wrongness. During a moment of self-reflexivity, Vargas ponders diverse itineraries prompted by his thematically recursive misrecognition as a Mexican:

> My thirty-sixth birthday was approaching, another year of being stuck in America. Since many assume I'm Mexican, I figured I should at least see Mexico, which is less than three hundred miles away from my apartment in downtown Los Angeles. But of course I couldn't go. I tried not using the word "stuck," but a careful review of my thesaurus yielded no suitable alternative. The word was "stuck," and I was stuck.[66]

While other moments of his biography foreground a migrant subjectivity that is in flux and characterized by a transience that does not permit durable queer sexual intimacy, he reluctantly arrives at a self-understanding that is qualitatively and factually stuck. It is important to note that this is a material stuckness that both is historically produced by and is a symptom of the colonial histories of US conquest of previously Mexican territories. His Filipinx identity is conditioned by a criminality produced by US immigration law, while also being hailed by the Mexican nation-state, whose current boundaries are themselves colonially manufactured. Like with his name, Vargas stunningly describes a displacement that he feels from a territory that he is not from, but to which he feels at least some level of connection. What does it mean to feel a level of nostalgia for a place from which you do not derive any ethnonational heritage, and yet the colonial geographies of which materially shape your body's identification? And what does it mean when the imprecise and racist field of racial (mis)identification that circumscribes one's embodiment also is in political dialogue with materially empirical histories of colonialism that have shaped the geographies upon which one's racialized subjectivity and identity navigate? It is an error that carries the epistemic weight of empirical truth. It is a misattribution that furnishes the heft of disorienting facticity. And it is this factual imprecision that ironizes the categorical imperatives of rationally delineated, ordered histories whose own inability to account cleanly for a Mexicanized Filipinx undocumented migrant are clarified.

This impreciseness surfaces via an important contradiction: Vargas is imminently deportable *and* stuck. While his brown embodiment ironically manifests a transient quality in a legal sense of undocumentation, it is also understood through a Borderlands geography that exceeds its precise origins. At the same time, it furnishes a specificity with regard to the borderized ideologies and imaginaries that shape racialized notions of migration in the United States. The ostensive Mexicanness of the non-Mexican Filipino exposes the layering of these geographies upon human experience, while arguably (given the colonial record) calling into question the incredulity of that ostensiveness. Mexico overdetermines his racial identification within a US racial imaginary, stressing a geographic milieu which exceeds him, while also displacing him—a displacement that creates the desire to entreat oneself to the space of Mexico as a return that is not a return. His body's citation of these extensive geographies travels further than his actual body can, superseding its boundaries, yet highlighting its legal boundedness. This double-bind results in an ironic racial determination of and through Mexicanness, as well as the expression of an unrequited desire to "at least see Mexico," as "many assume I'm Mexican."

This colonial kaleidoscope of misidentification dovetails with Vargas's definition of citizenship. Vargas's multiracialized citizen seems to elicit the kinds of cross-community coalition that my project envisions for Latinx and Filipinx studies, given the ways in which the Filipinx undocumented seems to find phantasmal ubication within multiple geographies of colonial encounter. Vargas receives a formal invitation from Nancy Pelosi to a joint session of Congress, which he considers with some trepidation, as it would put him on federal property. He ultimately accepts the invitation, as his conception of citizenship would not have allowed him to deny it:

> Because I am not a citizen by law or by birth, I've had to create and hold on to a different kind of citizenship . . . something more akin to a citizenship of anticipation. Citizenship is showing up. Citizenship is using your voice while making sure you hear other people around you. Citizenship is how you live your life. Citizenship is resilience.[67]

I home in on these various moments in Vargas's memoir because they constitute, at least partly, the diverse political and racial coordinates that shape his subjectivity. Very compellingly and in relation to the idea of Muñoz's brown commons is that Vargas actually provides us the tools and a primer through which to understand the mutual enmeshment of immigrant lives in the United States, despite the racial lenses we leverage that potentially obscure connection rather than emphasize it. As I have elaborated, his idea of passing is not an individualist one. Instead, one passes in a community and because of networks of support. As Judith Butler remarks in a conversation with disability artist-activist Sunaura

Taylor: one does not walk without a technique of walking. That is to say, there is a whole edifice and infrastructure that supports and undergirds one's act of walking, and indeed shapes the subjective volition of one's desire to even partake of a walk.[68] The same goes for passing.[69] There can be said to be a technique of passing, stitching together the lives of undocumented people intentionally in bonds of mutuality. As I have argued across this book, misrecognition is itself symptomatic of a mutually shared social location of racial disposability under racial capitalism. This renders the political crossings amongst Filipinx and Latinx lives an intriguing and significant proposition for racial coalition.

The comparative racial brownness of Latinx and Filipinx subjects draws critically on other histories of forced migration and displacement. It should be noted that histories of the transatlantic slave trade, settler colonialism, the global coolie trade, and transpacific expansion, while part of distinct events in the various movements of humanity, are all emblematic of global colonial processes that shape Filipinx and Latinx migration and diasporic identity. These global processes of colonialism are palimpsestically scripted under US citizenship, and ironically give impetus to the multiracial affinities under liberal racial capitalism that occasion Vargas's anxiety over misrecognition. The racial passing as Mexican furtively highlights, as I have been elaborating, a shared condition of colonial encounter, shaping subjects that have been innervated by colonial violence from Spain and the US. Misrecognition and the racial uncanny that it produces are experiences symptomatic of a shared colonial social location under the vicissitudes of racial capital. Once more, their histories of migration braid in lands that were once part of the Spanish empire, then transformed into US territories. These expansions of Manifest Destiny eventually led to the US's century of transpacific empire building that then saw the subsequent assimilation of the Philippines as US territory once also previously a part of the Spanish *ultramar*. Vargas's sense of identity and its emplacement in the Borderlands space of California begins his autobiographical exploration of self. Texas is the place in which this exploration ends, staging a powerful moment of dysphoric misrecognition embedded in a space of borderized carcerality.

In a chapter entitled "Detained," Vargas details his experience in a detention facility in southern Texas in 2014. In the chapter, he describes a sullen scene of dehumanization, in which he is actually detained with twenty-five children between five and twelve years old. We will later learn that he was imprisoned with children, instead of with other adult men, because he was being hidden by border agents from the eyes of the press that were touring the facility. The scene is dysphoric for another reason, punctuated by the consistent refrain of "If I spoke Spanish" worth quoting at length:

> If I spoke Spanish, I could have told the boys not to be scared.
>
> If I spoke Spanish, I could have told the boys about Ellis Island. About how the very first person in line on the opening day of America's first immigration station—an unaccompanied minor named Annie Moore who traveled on a steamship from Ireland—was someone just like them. Except she was white, before she knew she was white.
>
> If I spoke Spanish, I could have told the boys that none of this was their fault. I could have made sure they understood—even if most Americans do not—that people like us come to America because America was in our countries.
>
> . . . How a trade agreement, like the North American Free Trade Agreement, drove millions of Mexicans out of jobs and led parents to cross borders and climb up walls so they could feed their kids. How six decades of interventionist policies by both Republicans and Democrats brought economic and political instability and sowed violence in El Salvador, Guatemala, and Honduras. If I spoke Spanish, I could have explained, in the clearest, most accessible way I could, the connection between the dirty, muddy, worn-out Reeboks and Nikes they were wearing inside that cell and the inherent American need to expand its economic and political empire. I could have drawn a line between what used to be called "imperialism"—justified by "Manifest Destiny," "the White Man's Burden," and American's desire to "discover" new "frontiers"—to what is now known as "internationalism" and "globalization."[70]

This scene provides for us an encounter of obstructed communication punctuated with the myriad reflections—perhaps melancholic—on Vargas's inability to speak in Spanish. This moment is brought to us by the carceral regimes of US border security; however, subtending this encounter are the markedly different life trajectories of the detainees. These young boys are likely Central American refugees fleeing violence due in part to the imperial interventionist policies that Vargas details at length. Intriguingly, he provides this information to his readers that he cannot to the children, highlighting the linguistically inhibited pedagogy of the scene. While their lives are different, all the people in that cell migrated, though with varying and asymmetrical degrees of volition, against their will. The subjectivities of the adults around them were shaped by complex economic and political processes that narrowed the band of choice left to them. We can engage the adaptive and multifariously constrained arena of free will and agency available to migrants who were left to the vicissitudes of racial capitalism's exploitations, while also simultaneously enumerating an entire security apparatus and legal infrastructure against some of the most marginal beings in the world—children, who are both victims of political circumstance and convenient political chess pieces in the liberal machine of exclusivist citizenship.

Even so, Vargas has a completely different life, residing in the United States despite his undocumented status. These marked differences in social and economic class might drive a distinctive wedge between the entirely manufactured destitution of these Central American children caused by the destabilizing presence of the US in the Americas, on the one hand, and the objective positioning of Vargas within an international and global middle class, on the other. Nevertheless, that these striking differences exist within the same carceral space engineered by the US security state is a crucial detail in articulating a comparative cross-racial politics of affinity and intention toward another. The alterity of these Central American children, paired with the itinerant habits of mind cultivated by Vargas throughout his life, helps to materialize an attempt to inhabit the "worn-out Reeboks and Nikes" of another. This is a material difference and embodied presence that would scarcely arrive in any significant way before the eyes of another whose life has not been so dramatically shaped by the racial-economic processes of which *Dear America* gives at least a partial inventory. The fact that the Philippines, Mexico, and Central America can inhabit the same colonial manufactured carceral space itself indexes the varied and diverse cartographies that subtend the detention cell.

Vargas's melancholic and suspended transferal of knowledge to the young boys—a melancholia emblematized by his hapless inability to speak Spanish—is a moment of pedagogical encounter that is not an isolated, historically discrete event. Rather, I strongly suggest that it occasions a productive rupture in the linear narrativization of migrant movement, exposes the latticed networks of encounter that migration can elicit, and elaborates modes of multivocal address that themselves are historically shaped by the vicissitudes of Spanish and US colonial racial violences. Such vicissitudes are enumerated even further with this exchange, in which we learn Jose Antonio Vargas's true name:

> I told the boy: "*No hablo español.*" Quickly, I added, "*Soy filipino.*" I am Filipino: a declaration that seemed to cause more confusion to the

> young boy holding the crunched-up [Mylar] blanket. I'm not sure he heard me when I said, almost in a whisper, like a prayer, "*Pepeton ang pangalan ko*." My name is Pepeton.[71]

In a narrative in which the thematic importance of Jose's non-accented name has been recurrent, this belated introduction near the end of Vargas's memoir is evocative. In a way, he meets himself in this cell in a moment of vertiginous racial uncanny. We learn that this name is a "sobriquet" that was used during his time in the Philippines. While not a name of endearment, it was "the name of my past"—it is a portmanteau common in many Filipino naming practices whose familiar Hispanized parts (Jose, hence "Pepe"; Antonio, thus "Ton") index modes both of relation and of address inflected by Spanish colonialism.[72] These resonate as a mode of relation within the space of the carceralized border, facilitating an axis of affinity that simultaneously exposes colonial processes for their global reach, and yet anchors in the particular criminalities that attach to the brown, illegal body. Thus, it is not too much of a stretch that he would see himself in a Central American boy who he is so unlike, but with whom he is collapsed in a US multiracial imaginary. This imaginary, naturally and surreptitiously, has long historical legs.

The ways that Vargas makes sense of the tensions of assimilation and imperial statecraft are partly templated by Rudyard Kipling's poem "The White Man's Burden: The United States and the Philippines Islands," which he indeed cites. It describes the hapless natives of the Philippine islands through infantilizing rhetorics of developmentalism in which they were ever "silent [and] sullen peoples" and "half devil and half child."[73] Vargas historically is that bedeviled "half child" who now sees himself reflected in the face of a Central American migrant child. These modes of address and affinity emerge as instructive and dense nodes of contact within the US border security apparatus. This is a pivotal point, as it grounds Vargas's understanding of how the destinies of these young boys and his own intertwined. This, to me, evokes an important connection demonstrative of what M. Jacqui Alexander has summoned through and as "pedagogies of crossing." Alexander demonstrates the ways that infelicitous circumstances paradoxically occasion providential relationalities that can offer heterodox modes of analysis and coalition that disrupt "inherited boundaries of geography, nation, episteme and identity."[74]

Vargas remarks that, in order "[t]o understand how the boys and I ended up inside that jail cell, you must unravel a vast enforcement apparatus that is part police force, part frontier cavalry, part deportation machine, and altogether unprecedented in immigration history."[75] This passage appears in a chapter following his descriptions of being incarcerated along the border. It gives the reader much-needed context on the realities of US border enforcement—typically an abstraction in the minds of most. Such context circles around the particularities of Texas. Anthropologist Jason De León has described with gruesome detail the US policy of "prevention through deterrence."[76] This was a concerted effort by the United States government to divert the flow of migrants from "the suburbs of San Diego and El Paso toward treacherous mountains and deserts."[77] It has had disastrous effects. Now migrants often pass through the Sonoran Desert along the Arizona border—a corridor of violence and death. De León argues that the US intentionally uses the caustic environment and terrain of the desert to discourage illegal passage, while also intimately understanding the high likelihood of migrant death for those desperate enough to attempt the crossing. If they die in the desert, then the US has a convenient way to deflect blame and accusations of human rights violations by placing the blame on the desert environment itself as a non-human aggressor against human life and dignity. Mexican and Central American deaths in this desert landscape constitute crimes without perpetrators. Vargas reflects as much, striking an important affective chord with his readership in a move that is evocative of what I have been elaborating as rhetorical techniques of undocumentality:

> Whether you call them migrants, immigrants, or refugees, their journeys included an arduous trek through desert terrain. Often, they lacked food, water, and shelter. Many arrived dehydrated and hungry. Some required medical attention. Once they crossed the Rio Grande, they didn't try to hide from Border Patrol agents. They walked up to the officers and gave themselves up.[78]

While in Texas, the conditions to which the migrants were subjected and the political realities of their passage clearly demonstrate the cruel racial calculus of border securitization that characterizes "prevention through deterrence." Like many moments in Vargas's memoir, the racialized politics of disability are imminently relevant here, with these children arriving in a debilitated state—disabilities that are orchestrated by the US racial state. It is the state that predisposes broad swaths of racialized migrants to injury in order to shore up an able-bodied citizenry and ableist form of nationalism. These dynamics are further exacerbated by the extent to which, as has been discussed previously, the United States and its citizenry have historically relied on the able-bodied labor power of alien non-citizens as a mechanism of wealth generation.

## Conclusion: The Racial Error of Solidarity

Vargas establishes the interdependence elicited by racial passing and misrecognition as an alternative mode of horizontal comradeship constitutive of an imagined community.[79] I have elaborated upon the ways that the continuum of passing, via Vargas's own elaboration of the racial ambiguity occasioned by Filipinx identity, provides an exciting and indispensable template for thinking through comparative racialization. The suspended agency marked by Filipinx ambiguity and misrecognition paradoxically implicates an exciting heuristic that runs against the grain of an ostensive identity empiricism that can overdetermine ethnic studies and political activism, and thus stifle coalitional praxis. The comfort of empirical, monolithic, and discrete identities derives its power via their disinvestment from the non-catharsis of racial ambivalence. That is to say, ambiguity is not convenient for political projects that rely on empirically stable identities. These disinvestments reproduce identity structures that can unknowingly reinforce a state power predicated on a biopolitical knowledge of the populations it governs through intimate knowledge of their identities.[80] The state thrives on fixity, which itself is emblematized by the disciplinizing comfort of documentation. Chandan Reddy analyzes the relationship of state power's assumption as the seat of "freedom" through the obfuscated subterranean realities of its own rationalizing "violence" as pivoting around the state's continued ability to enter the business of subjectivity.[81] Filipinx ambivalence offers pathways to resist this business. This ambivalence is not a consequnce of an uncritical embrace of racial collapse with the other, but rather the measured relation with another who, for deeply embedded and often misunderstood reasons, you are cast as being like. Muñoz's brown commons gives a meaningful sense of this abstractive personhood that is navigated by Vargas. This is a navigation, I suggest, of the vicissitudes of undocumented personhood as it is itself complexified by the concrete experience of misrecognition.

Given these intercalated histories, it seems less surprising that there would indeed be racial misrecognition (how could there not be?)—a symptomatic phenomenon of the mutual interposition of Latinx and Filipinx Americans. Vargas's text furnishes a mode through which racial error might constitute the very prime material for racial solidarity. These "erroneous" affinities constitute ones that, in line with Muñoz's idea of a brown commons, may point to liminal subject positions that exceed the seductive structure of national citizenship. It is ironic, perhaps, when misrecognition in the present—the erroneous collapsing of one's self into the subject position of another—is an error that points to an archive of factual, mutually-shared colonial interactions that might not be substantively engaged with otherwise. What if such affective and identitarian indeterminacy were engaged with for a little bit longer, rather than coming to a premature yet cathartic resolution through citizenship—which, in part, relies on the state knowing precisely who you are? I am suggesting that racial indeterminacy and ambivalence represent thwarted identity empiricism, which potentiates the diagnosis of the colonial conditions that shape that very indeterminacy's possibility in the first place. This evasion of empiricism represents an epistemic heuristic I have been theorizing as the racial uncanny of dos x rooted paradoxically in a Filipinx subjectivity that is uncanny unto itself.

# 4 | Mad Migrant Imaginary

## *Asian American and Latinx Disability Politics in Translation*

*Undone* is a television series that first aired in 2019, created and written by Raphael Bob-Waksburg and Kate Purdy.[1] Directed by Dutch director Hisko Hulsing, the show artfully explores the "elastic nature of reality" through the perspective of its Mexican American Deaf and schizophrenic protagonist, Alma Winograd-Díaz, portrayed by Peruvian-Canadian actress Rosa Salazar (pictured on the next page). The show's photography and cinematography feature the artistic use of rotoscoping, an animation technique in which live action footage is traced over frame by frame with artistic, lively, animation art. This chapter will feature many images from the show displaying this technique. Alma navigates a surreal rotoscoped transition from deaf to hearing, while also experiencing the onset of symptoms consistent with schizophrenia. The show's plot centers around investigating the events surrounding her father's (Jacob Winograd) death when she was a child, with Alma also coming to understand the nature of her father's neuroscientific research on schizophrenia. The show establishes Alma's experience of both her deafness and neurodivergence as bound up with an exploration of her racial mestiza identity. Moreover, the nonlinear and disjointed ways that she explores this identity open up the limited geographies through which Mexican migrant identity is typically understood. I argue that this opens comparative pathways that connect Latinx and Asian American migrant subjectivities across language, space, and time, demonstrating that disability enhances a comparative ethnic studies analysis materializing through what I call a "mad migrant imaginary."[2] I take up Alicia R. Schmidt Camacho's tremendous concept, placing it in explicit conversation with disability politics. However, these migrant identities and imaginaries intersect within the colonial space of the US-Mexico Borderlands, displacing Indigenous peoples, and thus coinciding migration with settler colonial processes.

While this chapter is methodologically and primarily one of cultural analysis, because of the ways that biomedical and neuroscientific knowledge is treated in *Undone*, it is relevant to gain at least a cursory understanding of the environmental and psychological risk factors that contribute to the diagnosis of schizophrenia. However, it is important to note that this is a medicalized and scientific understanding of the condition, and thus represents one framework to understand it. The *Diagnostic and Statistical Manual of Mental Disorders (DSM-5)* defines schizophrenia as existing on a spectrum of intensity and variety of psychotic disorders, all of which involve some combination of "delusions, hallucinations, disorganized thinking (speech), grossly disorganized or abnormal motor behavior (including catatonia), and negative symptoms."[3] In *Psychodynamic Psychiatry in Clinical Practice*, Dr. Glen O. Gabbard observes schizophrenia was psychoanalytically described as a problem with *cathexis*.[4] Sigmund Freud defined cathexis as the mental process by which subjects invested psychic or libidinal energy in objects—an investment that modern theorists would likely describe as attachment. When we form attachments to objects or people, we invest psychic energy in them, fueling and cultivating that

**Figure 1.** *Alma having a hallucinatory episode. The southwestern sky behind her is painted beige and teal. The image evokes the animation technique of rotoscoping, characterized by sharp comic book–like lines, two-dimensionality, and matte coloring.*

FIGURE 2. *Alma schizophrenically travelling through time and space. Her father is surreally suspended in the air.*

connection. In the realm of schizophrenia, Freud theorized that, rather than forming attachments to "improper" objects (as in homosexuality), schizophrenics experienced decathexis or a withdrawal from objects/people around them, followed by a subsequent *cathexis* that directed inward, "reinvested in the self or ego."[5] It should be noted that there are gender-based biases in this Freudian take, which almost wholly blamed the etiology of the condition on the poor care from "schizophrenogenic mothers," describing the most severe cases as withdrawing so deeply within the self to the point of delusion—thus crafting a highly individuated reality thoroughly detached from shared experience with the rest of the world.[6]

In this chapter, I disidentify with the epistemological shuffle of im/proper object choice and cathexis in psychiatric understandings of schizophrenia in order to argue that it is impossible to understand an economy of disability and its managements disarticulated from the intersecting landscapes of race, immigration, and assimilation. *Undone* provides us a cultural archive in which we can ask and answer related questions about this interplay of factors, arriving at what many scholars like Jina B. Kim, Sami Schalk, and Eunjung Kim have variously advanced as a "crip-of-color critique," a "feminist of color disability studies," or "postcolonial disability studies"—essentially placing the racial analysis of disability that attends to the effects of racial capitalism, settler colonialism, and transnational differences in the experience of impairment.[7]

Something somewhat contrary to the settler history of psychiatry emerges in *Undone*.[8] Similarly evocative of the ways that settler society and the confinement of the "mad" intertwine, we are led to believe that Alma, who exhibits the symptomology of someone with schizophrenia, is actually coming into her own Indigenous shamanic powers. In this way, western science and the empirical substantiation of her mental capacities as extraordinary (rather than invariably debilitating) do work to indigenize Alma. That is, Indigenous subjects emerge at various moments of the story, providing the "empirical" evidence of the true nature of schizophrenia. It is established that Alma's mestizaje as a Mexican American woman places her in an Indigenous genealogy of shamanic forbearers, establishing it as almost a birthright. Such seemingly Indigenous ties in her mestiza consciousness are consistently established in her various interactions with Indigenous peoples in the southwestern United States.[9] Nevertheless, the specious assumption of a mutually shared Indigenous spiritual worldview between Mexican Americans and Indigenous peoples that is foregrounded in the show requires intentional unpacking. In the section that follows, I explore the experience of racialized deafness, before elaborating a transnational vista of comparative racial analysis intertwining Latinx and Asian American migrant subjectivities. Both these analyses are attentive to the intersecting racialized politics of linguistic self-determination, accents, and psychonormalization.

## Mad Deaf

The adult Alma that we first meet in the show possesses the ability to speak a seemingly unobstructed oral English that you might expect from the "normal" speech of the hearing. We noticeably observe that Alma is able to hear because of the use of a surgically installed cochlear implant, which we later learn in the show was acquired at the insistence of her mother, Camila Díaz. A conventional reading attending to the differential and asymmetrical effects of "audism," or a form of ableism in which hearing people and culture are prioritized, would suggest that Camila is in the wrong for insisting that Alma conform to normality for her able-bodied comfort.[10] Literature in Deaf[11] studies and politics affirm that, since there exists a robust system of American Sign Language, it is not advisable to surgically alter a deaf child's body and, instead, they should learn to communicate in sign.[12] Deafness in this perspective is benign and a valid human physical difference. Moreover, "correcting" it is an affront to Deaf culture—even genocidal. Parents should follow suit accommodating their child's difference, rather than insisting upon conformity with able-bodied hearing culture—so the arguments go. We learn that Camila, however, wanted to be able to communicate with her daughter vocally and to make it easier for Alma to assimilate into American culture as the child of an immigrant. Is Camila prioritizing the needs, ease, and experiences of hearing people over those of her daughter, who could explore her identity as a Deaf person in the Deaf community?

As a child enrolled in a Deaf school, Alma has found community and friendship. On her mother's recommendation, she is pulled out of the school, and Alma is forced to say goodbye to her deaf friends. The scene of her departure from the school is quite moving, and one gets the impression that the mother, in her eagerness for her daughter to begin her "normal" life with her, sees neither the friendships that her daughter has made with other deaf children to be worthy of cultivation, nor that they would have even enriched Alma's life in any meaningful way. Instead, they are perhaps representative of the difference that Alma must overcome and leave behind in order to assimilate into American culture as an effective citizen. These deaf characters never again appear in the show, which centers around hearing people frankly sidestepping the agency of the Deaf. It would have been innovative to hold hearing and Deaf identities more in relation, particularly through the presence of consistent signing alongside oral speech. Instead, Alma is normalized, and the show's linguistic landscape is largely governed by oral English. The racial dynamics between Spanish and English in the Southwest and the Winograd-Díaz family complicate this critical reading, however. To assume wholly that Alma's is an uncomplicated ableist narrative transformation that centers the hearing would disregard the fact that ASL and English are not the only two languages that inform this disability context.

In a particularly evocative moment, Jacob suggests that Camila learn ASL in order to adapt to her daughter's difference, rather than enforce normalization through medical intervention. Camila retorts, "Why don't you learn Spanish?" This highlights that the logics of normalization and rehabilitation are not linear and are, instead, embedded in a complicated political ecology that asks that we consider the relationship of multiple languages, assimilation, citizenship, migration, and colonial history. It may also present a suggestive critique of the whiteness of Deaf culture, which might not consider the additional negotiations of Deaf people of color in balancing an ethnic heritage and their cultural attachments to deafness that may very well demand their rejection of such a heritage, if it means conforming to hearing culture. For a heritage speaker of Spanish who is deaf, there may be many linguistic parallels that this intersectional identity can pinpoint between Spanish and ASL, and that might go unacknowledged otherwise. Certain aspects of a critique of audism may persist with regard to Alma's normalization, but one may ask the reasonable question of why per se should maintenance of ASL take precedence over Spanish?

While certain features of the critique of ableism and audism in Alma's assimilation into able-bodied society are compelling and should not be dismissed out of hand, it is important to point out that an insistence on prioritizing Deaf culture at the political expense of hearing tout court would fundamentally inhibit Alma's access to Spanish—clearly an important marker of linguistic identity and connection with Camila and Mexican heritage. This is frankly not unlike English-only mandates in schools or workplaces directed at Spanish speakers. While the desire to affirm Deaf culture and identity in the United States vis-à-vis the dominant political language of English would prompt a disidentification with the uncritical demands of exclusively centering the needs and comfort of hearing individuals, these demarcated lines of power are not as clear in ASL's relation to Spanish. For all intents and purposes, Deaf culture revolves around the maintenance and flourishing of ASL, which might ironically come at the expense of the linguistic and racial diversity of Deaf people of color. We may not want to measure the gains and preservation of a robust Deaf culture by unintentionally colluding with the draconian, culturally anti-Mexican metrics of an immigrant-free American society that ignores its colonial history of land theft from Mexico. In this sense, the history of Mexico-US relations ought to be a part of Deaf history.

Rather than Deaf identity functioning simply as a disability identity (which many Deaf individuals would find extremely problematic), the centrality of ASL renders Deaf politics much more like those of an ethnolinguistic minority. This is a crucial and often overlooked point with regard to Deaf identity, and would call into question the lumping together of Deaf and hard-of-hearing individuals into a monolithic disabled community. Deaf histories and studies are sometimes better understood not as "disability" histories, but rather as the histories of a linguistic and cultural minority. Though language sovereignty and maintenance implicate similar notions of accessibility to public life that shape the experience of many minority languages, it would be problematic to assume that the linguistic politics of a full-fledged language like ASL, with its own grammar, syntax, and sociolinguistic cultural dynamics, would be reducible to the complicated array of psychophysical variations associated with

FIGURE 3 *Camila Díaz with the subtitle "Why don't you learn Spanish?"*

disability communities. In this sense, there is a lot more in common between ASL and Spanish in terms of the ways that access and citizenship adjoin ethnolinguistic minoritization. Adhering to a strict hearing-deaf binary would not capture these symmetries between sign language and orally-spoken minority languages. Within the US-context, particularly around the border, precisely how much hearing privilege does Spanish have in relation to English? That is, in a context in which the speaking of Spanish can be a political liability for many, how much unfettered access to normate citizenship critiqued by disability advocates does it truly possess and garner?[13] And in the maintenance and proliferation of Deaf culture, to include someone like Alma, would it be too much to ask that she give up Spanish and this important cultural connection with her mother?

I would suggest that a systematic critique of hearing privilege in culture must consider various aspects of racial difference and respect for the ethnolinguistic identities of other racial minorities in any critical account of ableism. That is to say, in a political environment like the United States, in which English is the prestige language, Spanish has a subordinate position—one that presents certain obstacles that mirror those of ASL-speakers' navigation of hearing society. While the relationship of Spanish to English is not reducible or equivalent to disability, there are certainly a series of disabling effects with regard to consistent access to education, services, citizenship, and other privileges. And while it is clearly the case that hearing culture is prioritized in *Undone*, with the consistent presence of signing phased out narratively, Spanish is essentially completely absent. Beyond a few stray words, Alma does not produce the consistent meaning in Spanish that she does in ASL. In this sense (while narrow, it is significant), Spanish may have a subordinate position to ASL, thus speaking directly to the marginalized position of Camila (Alma's mother) in the entire linguistic arrangement both of the Winograd-Díazes and of the US side of the Borderlands generally. This places her insistence on hearing—so Alma can learn Spanish and assimilate into US culture in ways that she is prohibited from doing completely as a Mexican immigrant—in a much more holistic context that better elaborates Alma's subjectivity as not completely capitulating to audist privilege.

In the next section, I seek to further complicate the reading I present above by foregrounding the ways that a mad migrant cultural imaginary demonstrates how disability analysis profoundly enriches comparative race critique. *Undone* aids us in articulating lines of transnational affinity between Asian Americans and Latinx Americans, with a particular regard for South Asian and Mexican American connection across geography, difference, and language.

## Cripping Accents across Geography: Asian American and Latinx Migrant Imaginaries

Earlier in this chapter, I mentioned the ways that clinical and diagnostic discourses have understood the psychopathology of schizophrenia partially as an issue of *cathexis*, which describes the process by which we invest energy into objects or people. Schizophrenia in a Freudian model has been described as decathexis, or the withdrawal from social reality outside of the self, and reinvestment into one's own ego to the point of delusion.[14] I revisit these more clinical discourses with a cultural studies contribution. What I want to bring to these conversations is an understanding of the ways that the idea of decathexis amplifies the conversation from proper and improper psychic object choice to the narrative explication of racial immigrant identity, as it enfolds through the prism of mental disability. Withdrawing into the self to the point of delusion is a process explored in *Undone* in ways that innovatively binds migrant subjectivity to others, i.e., telling the manifold stories and journeys of migration, rather than relying on ethnically siloed representations. Rather than decathexis being a withdrawal into the self that is then lost to reality, it is presented as an opening up of migrant subjectivity orienting the self toward the other. Instead of the propriety of object attachment, we see a cathexis that re-signifies the boundaries of migrant subjectivity in a multiperspectival orientation in relation to both South Asian and Mexican American migrant realities that do not typically overlap. The show beautifully threads the parallel assimilatory realties of Latinx and Asian American identities. The comparative move in the show transpires through the ways that disability identity navigates the politics of accents and colonial subjectification. This intersectionality comes through as a quality of storytelling. The narrative structure utilizing schizophrenia as an alternative storytelling technique that plays with time and linearity, and embraces unreason as a solid basis for the examination of reality, thus facilitates a connection between two migrant stories from vastly different geographies—stories that connect in a moment of linguistic intimacy. Disability becomes the scaffold underwriting transnational multiracial affinities through language.

The show provides an incredibly rich portrayal of immigration and assimilation and their intersection with disability. A remarkably important character in this regard is Alma's boyfriend, Sam, portrayed by Indian-American actor Siddharth Dhananjay. Sam, for his part, aids in Alma's post-accident investigation into the circumstances of her father's death and the contents of his controversial research program. Sam importantly bears witness to many of Alma's special abilities to intuit personal details about the lives of others that she should not otherwise know. Much of the show is somewhat ambivalent about the veracity of Alma's preternatural perception abilities (are they real or a product of her psychosis?), but moments with Sam seem to lend credence to them. These abilities and temporal jumps into the past shed light on Sam's migrant subjectivity in a truly moving and beautiful portrait of Asian American and Latinx affinities.

We discover that Sam is a 1.5 generation immigrant and that he and his family are from Sri Lanka. We make this discovery through an unexpected source: Alma's schizophrenia. During one of her hallucinatory episodes, in which she is seemingly traveling through time and space, she encounters a childhood version of Sam in his past, before he arrived in the United States. He is playing with two of his friends and they all are speaking in South-Asian-accented English, with some Tamil interspersed. Alma witnesses the scene perplexed, perhaps noting how different this Sam is from the one that we have come to know. The present-day Sam speaks in an "accentless" (or should we say an Americanized accented) English—a "normal" prestige variety that you might find spoken in

California, the Midwest, or parts of the Northeast. Sam's mother arrives, instructing him to say goodbye to his friends, as the family will be moving to the US. His friends are surprised, as Sam did not share any details of his departure, likely not wanting to come to terms with leaving. In a scene symmetrical to Alma leaving her deaf school, Sam painfully says goodbye to his childhood friends, thus leaving his home and everything he once knew. This symmetry between Sam with his accented English and Alma with her deafness draws a powerful connection between disability, migration, and language that is, from my vantage, exceptionally unique in cultural production.

Alma jumps forward in time to Sam as a new immigrant in elementary school. Two boys bully Sam mercilessly for his heavy accent. In a deeply profound and moving scene for its implications, Alma again jumps through time and encounters childhood Sam in his bedroom listening to playback of American-accented English. Crestfallen, he trains his mouth and tongue to mimic the sounds painstakingly and in a repetitious manner. We are treated to the profound lessons that many accented immigrant children learn, having to make the traumatic choice to eclipse differences that are viewed by US society as deficiencies. While not as extreme as cochlear surgery to enhance hearing, Sam's use of recording technology and playback to modify the ways that his body naturally works in order to produce sounds that are unfamiliar to him is rather notable.

**FIGURE 4** *Sam as a child seated on his bed listening to recordings of "standard" English.*

To use the oft-quoted phrase: he tamed his wild tongue, and this taming is mediated by and through a form of technological intervention.[15] Alma realizes that Sam went through a similar process of linguistic assimilation into English. Although Sam already spoke English, it was the rehabilitation of his accent that marked his normalization, and it was his accent per se that marked his deficiency. Despite much of the sub-continent of Asia experiencing centuries-long rule of British imperialism, and the fact that it is one of the largest Anglophone populations in the world, US racialized animus against immigrants compounds harm in this instance by obfuscating this colonial history and the valid variety of English that emerges from it. Why should English be seen as the property of the inheritors of one British colony in North America over the descendants of one British colony in South Asia? An English that is Sam's by right, as the descendent of the colonial violence that Anglophonized his nation, is disarticulated and dispossessed from him. There are a number of aspects to remark upon here that challenge a hearing/Deaf and disability/able-bodied binary in making sense of migration, race, and linguistic colonialism. In short, this encounter across the geographies of accent manifests through a shared vulnerability produced through the racialized optics of who is deemed a proper, healthy Anglophone citizen-subject. Moreover, in this transnational encounter across accent, language, and experience, it is Alma's acquired ability to hear that allows us to take stock of the global effects of disablement, which unexpectedly connects the British colonial experience of Sri Lanka with the US colonial experience of the Mexican American Borderlands through the prism of normative English and deviations from it.

The position of South Asian history, migration, and subjectivity has been a vital field of inquiry in understanding United States immigration history. While Asian American scholarship on the "coolie" global labor market in the nineteenth century can often be synonymous with a history of Chinese migrant diaspora, South Asian labor was also a constitutive part of this market that eventually shifted the racial maps of the Americas. There has also been recent work commenting on the intersecting subject positions of Latinx and South Asian Americans in the realm of sexuality and performance cultures. Kareem Khubchandani has argued that middle- to upper-class South Asian migrants to the United States often navigate their way through multinational racial capitalism through accented performance that actually accentuates their difference from white heteronormativity, rather than inclusion into it.[16] Oftentimes, this has caused, as Khubchandani observes ethnographically, misrecognition and identity slippage between South Asian and Latinx subjects. He accounts for this by using José Esteban Muñoz's notions of brown affect, feeling, and politics.[17] I, like Khubchandani, am very interested in these slippages, interconnections, and unexpected affinities where brown maps onto brown in a multiracial American imaginary. This is not only an affective relation in the contemporary moment; Mexican American and South Asian American intersections also have deep-seated articulations connecting the migration histories from Mexico and South Asia to the United States. For instance, historian of race and sexuality Nayan Shah has demonstrated that when migrant men from India married Mexican American women (as they often did), the two partners would be marked as the "same race" by county clerks issuing marriage licenses, and therefore these Indian-Mexican unions were not in violation of anti-miscegenation laws of the early twentieth century. Under US structures, South Asians and Mexicans were legally considered—at least in the context of heterosexual marriage—not racially distinct.[18] It is therefore intriguing that in contemporary culture like that of *Undone* we see cultural resonances of these historical affinities or, in juridical spheres, legal racial sameness.

I suggest that what Alma and Sam's encounter communicates to us is that colonialism transpires across a racialized sensorium, articulating a kind of transnational "stranger intimacy," to use Shah's formulation, that challenges the balkanized tendencies that can structure engagements with immigration history. Moreover, it is Alma's subjectivity as a disabled woman of color that ensures a resistance to "alienation" and articulates a "desire for visceral solidarity."[19] Had Alma not acquired the ability to hear, however, she would not have been able to understand Sam's struggles, as she would not have been able to hear the different accents and the ways in which these shape different Englishes. Beyond reading about them, she would not have been able to sonically experience a very important transnational connection across the different accented geographies that compose US migration and assimilation. Neither could we comprehend the ways that colonial histories from other contact zones are exacerbated within what would initially be surmised as narrowly domestic matters of Americanization. In this instance, her ability to hear actually enhances her disability identity and, specifically, the affinities through which her Deafness can articulate across racial and linguistic difference. Indeed, the oral English from which Deaf culture and ASL might disidentify is not monolithic and has complex colonial legacies that subtend it. Moreover, her ability to distinguish vocal accent, and thus to empathize with Sam's emotional labor in mimetically adjusting his mouth and tongue, actually allows her to place her Deaf identity (as she underwent similar processes of normalization into English) within a larger context that includes the realities of Asian American migration, exclusion, and assimilation. In this sense, the accented bridge connecting Sam and Alma's migrant subjectivities is facilitated by her ability to hear, while her ability to empathize with an equivalent experience of linguistic normalization is fundamentally rooted in her experience as a disabled woman of color.[20] Even as a hearing person in possession of all the privileges afforded within a society that prioritizes and structures itself around this ability, someone like Alma still bears the disenfranchisements and disablements that constitute racialized experience.

In a powerful way that productively draws upon the cognitive transience of migration and schizophrenia, the encounter between Sam and Alma mirrors what Shah describes as "the paradox of stranger intimacy . . . [which] offers a way of conceptualizing everyday encounters that can either invest in sustaining hierarchy or produce egalitarian social and political arenas, ethics, and associations."[21] My point here is that the linguistic and migrant affinities that are movingly shared between Asian American and Latinx cultures, to which Alma bears witness through one of her schizophrenic episodes, would not have been able to materialize in the same ways without her ability to hear. And yet an appreciation for the ways South Asian American and Mexican American identities intersect here would have been impoverished without Alma's experience as a Deaf person. Or, rather, without an experience of acquiring hearing—and the subsequent acquisition of oral language as it would be experienced as a disabled immigrant woman of color—a vital cross-racial imaginary bridging colonialisms, language, and geography would not be able to emerge. So, it is not hearing per se that facilitates this appreciation of accents that I want to pinpoint. Instead, it is the experience of hearing through the perspective of disablement and its management that inaugurates an encounter, making meaning of the colonial politics of accent and linguistic normalization.

My intention is certainly not to place hearing ability over Deaf culture, but to show the creative and important ways that Deaf and hearing cultures can meaningfully connect across difference and linguistic colonial frames of reference. This dialectical interplay between deafness and hearing fundamentally reorients our appreciation of the affects and connectivity between the seemingly very different migrant subjects represented by Alma and Sam. This is not to underplay the real divisions and oppressive dynamics that exist between hearing and Deaf experience.

Nevertheless, in my opinion, the nuances of this multiracial encounter would not be captured and would otherwise be invisible. However, the assumptions upon which the narrative disturbances to normative time and geography rest are on the figure of a schizophrenic deaf woman of color, who is configured as a supercrip with preternatural abilities to time travel. These supercrip abilities similarly rest upon, recenter, and leave unquestioned the logics of mestizaje that can dip into settler colonial territory. Moreover, this supercrip status into which Alma is positioned relies on a configuration of Indigenous identity and spirituality as magical plot devices. The "magical Indian" articulates the mestiza supercrip as capacitated settler citizen.

## The Supercrip Mestiza: Mestizaje and Indigenous Temporality

In disability studies, the supercrip has been defined as a problematic trope in disability inspiration narratives—sometimes called "inspiration porn." Likely deriving from the popular comic book hero Superman, the supercrip describes an individual who, despite their physical or mental deficiencies, is able to perform supernatural feats that even able-bodied people would find difficult. However, oftentimes, disabled people are praised for simply performing everyday life activities, thus "reflecting low expectations about what a person with a disability can do."[22] Such excessive praise can be awkward as "[m]any individuals view their impairment as part of their identity and not something to overcome or defeat."[23] While certain individual stories about surmounting the odds can on their own be inspiring, these stories understood within a context of ableism are problematic for a few reasons. First, they reduce the experience of disability to one of personal overcoming, rather than telling the story of structural changes that need to be affected for all people to thrive, irrespective of bodily difference and capacity. Second, in these individual inspiration narratives, there is the logical implication that the "problem" of disability is one of willpower, grit, and determination, and that the individual person is responsible for their own problems. If a disabled person can win a gold medal, then certainly other disabled people have no real cause for complaint. This accentuates the myth of liberal individualism foundational to the ideology of the citizen; the citizen is—or, should be—radically self-sufficient, and should contribute to the advantage of all. Ethnic studies scholars like Lisa Lowe, Grace Kyungwon Hong, and

Mae M. Ngai demonstrate the logical fallacies of this kind of thinking, as the US citizen's abstract freedom and independence often rely on the material capacities of the alien non-citizen's invisible labor power.[24] A third issue is that these narratives can tend to present disabled people as cultural, or even supernatural, oddities, distancing us from examining real-world conditions in favor of extravagant stories of fantastical people removed from our everyday lives. In reality, disabled people are all around us. They are family members, friends, or colleagues whose needs and material conditions for full-fledged participation and flourishing in society often go ignored. The popularity of the supercrip trope implies we would rather consume fantastical, one-in-a-million kinds of cases than think about disabled people as a real community with particular needs.

These kinds of stories can play into racial fantasies, as we can see in *Undone*. Alma is a supercrip because she is a disabled person who possesses supernatural abilities of perception and even time travel due to her schizophrenia. This trope not only rehashes some of the problems I elaborate above, but also problematically intersects with settler colonial discourses, where the inspirational discourse mitigating the realities of disability through a "magical" or spectacular mode appropriates Indigenous beliefs as the raw material for narrative fantasy. In this case, the "supercrip mestiza," as I will name this archetype, relies on a "magical Indian" presence, which problematically plays on both Spanish and US settler colonial ideologies. This transpires through the confirmation of Alma's powers by authenticating her heritage through an Indigenous interlocutor. Playing on the eugenic logics of mestizaje, this magical Indian essence is projected as being a part of Alma—her unquestioned, untroubled, and unproblematic inheritance. While many mestizos could certainly draw genealogical, even genetic, connections to Indigenous patrimony, existing within the political field of Indianness as it has been constructed through settler regimes of dispossession, land expropriation, and delimited national sovereignty is quite different from being a Mexican American ethnic minority. As María Josefina Saldaña-Portillo has argued, this Anzaldúan variety of mestiza consciousness treats indigeneity as a pastiche grab bag of Indianness to be conveniently fastened to one's subjecthood, without orienting oneself intentionally to contemporary issues of an Indigenous elimination whose realities do not exist as abstract identity markers for Indians in the same way they do for the diffuse, theoretically sophisticated mestiza who is able to shuttle between worlds.[25] Part of this is complicated and aggravated by mestizaje.

Mestizaje is a racial logic at play in many Latin American countries (including Mexico) and has historically suggested that the national racial body would incorporate Indigenous people, correcting their deficiencies by blending them with European blood. The mestizo was born and was seen as the "cosmic race"—a new kind of human person that eugenically left behind the negative traits of indigeneity while accentuating their positive attributes—a kind of human engineering only possible through racial mixture. Whereas places like Mexico predicated nation-building and "better breeding" on the ostensible incorporation of Indians, the United States was much more known for segregationist policies that separated out people of color and discouraged miscegenation in order to preserve white purity.[26] Both kinds of racial states construct Indians and the Indigenous as communities that are relegated to a past to be supplanted by incorporation and/or genocide. Mexican ethnologist José Vasconcelos, in *La raza cósmica*, heralded the mestizo as the utopian future of humanity, positioning the Indian as an antiquated past to be transcended through selective reproduction.[27] In this sense, the mestizo is modern and avant-garde, while the Indian is barbaric, primitive, and savage. In the United States, the Indian is seen as a figure that is relegated to the colonial past, and thus it is imagined that there are currently no native peoples in the contemporary moment. Unlike in Mexico, they do not "live on" as incorporated into the national body. However, tokenistic aspects of Indigenous culture are preserved in white American fantasy, in the form of Indian sports iconography; the names of places and states; US Western films; and militaristic nominal appropriations, like the "Tomahawk" missile. So, the Indian is preserved either through a mixed-race body, i.e., the mestiza, or culturally, in tokenistic ways that enhance white dominance, rather than pose questions about rightful land ownership. In either instance, contemporary Indigenous people are disappeared and replaced as part of what scholars like J. Kēhaulani Kauanui—engaging with Patrick Wolfe—call the structure, rather than the singular event, of settler colonialism.[28] The future of the nation is mortgaged on the Indian being calcified in a past temporality and denied coevality with the present.

Mestizaje functions with disability, drawing on these settler temporalities in Alma's navigation of her cognitive difference. As I mentioned in the introductory section, Alma's father worked as a neuroscientist, researching the ways that schizophrenia was not a mental malady, but rather a supernatural power that allows those that experience it to perceive time differently. When Jacob returns to Alma as a vision or a ghost, he attempts to explain to his daughter that she has special abilities that indeed allow her to speak to him, though he has passed. US-Mexico racial relations and the structure of settler colonialism inform and shape the father's empirical efforts to diversify his understanding of schizophrenia. In montages of Jacob's research, the show establishes that he uses Indigenous research subjects who undergo brain scans, which he then compares to patients experiencing schizophrenia. It is revealed that Jacob dedicated his research program to studying the brain patterns of many Indigenous spiritual leaders who are understood in their respective cultural contexts as a kind of shaman or faith-healer and who, through special sight, are able to detect aspects of reality that are not readily captured by western empiricism. Surprisingly enough, though narratively expected, the "shamanic" brain pattern is virtually identical to a brain readout that would be consistent with a diagnosis of schizophrenia. The show postulates Indigenous cultures' celebration of such individuals as healers and sages, while western cultures medicate, marginalize, and institutionalize.[29] Alma is at the intersection of these competing realities of western empiricism and Indigenous spirituality, allowing us to attribute to her a mestiza consciousness that must navigate the contradictory signs of the Borderlands—a subject position first popularized by Gloria Anzaldúa.[30]

Although it is possible to infer an affirmative reading of the ways that Indigenous knowledge can update western biomedical science's understanding of mental disabilities, it is also reasonable to question whether or not *Undone* succumbs to tokenization of Indigenous peoples, who are a "magical" plot device that diversifies western understandings of disability, while neglecting Indigenous people themselves. Disability historian and Deaf studies scholar Susan Burch has demonstrated the ways that settler colonialism and institutionalization have a deeply entwined history in the biopolitical management of the marginalized. Drawing on the work of Jessica Cowing and her framework of "settler ableism," Burch argues

> Beliefs in superiority and practices of domination—inherent aspects of settler colonialism—regularly invoke ableist logics. Through the lenses of normality, fitness, and competency, settlers have judged Indigenous people and nations. Historically, settlers have interpreted Native people's unwillingness or inability to conform to colonial ideals, such as individuality, heterosexuality, and materialism, as indications of inherent deficiencies or defects.[31]

That is, oftentimes psychiatric institutionalization of Indigenous people actively promoted and exacerbated both settler colonialism and the assertion of settler power over Indigenous life and minds. Alongside historians like Burch, disability studies scholars such as Geoffrey Reaume, Anna Mollow, La Marr Jurelle Bruce, and Therí Alyce Pickens theorizing in the realm of cognitive disability have come to understand western psychiatric categories as fabrications reflecting colonial or chauvinistic cultural values that are historically rooted in racism, and not transcendent normative ideals of the way a mind ought to be.[32] Moreover, western biomedical science would often diagnose symptoms and disabilities of Indigenous peoples that were likely the result of colonialism and native dispossession.[33] These often included symptoms of malaise, depression, hysteria, or substance abuse in the form of alcoholism.

Rather than focus on these historical realities, the use of Indigenous people to center the experiences of a mestiza woman to substantiate her as a magical character endowed with powers, rather than shine a light on the deep-seated traumas that psychonormalization has had on the Indigenous psyche could be seen as opportunistic and politically lacking. This critique materializes as even more convincing when we consider the ways that Jacob's research often used Native people as props giving evidentiary support for his cutting-edge and progressive views on mental disability. The Indigenous people that appear in the show appear without much nuance or depth, and lack specificity. When they do appear, they are more extensions of Alma's mestiza consciousness.

The connection is further substantiated later in Alma's life when

**FIGURE 5** *Alma in blue, speaking with an Indian dancer, who asks her if she is a "mestiza."*

she interacts with an Indigenous dancer who is performing a dance she calls "La Antigua" at an event in a hotel conference room. "La Antigua" is a dance that is meant to call upon the ancestors. Alma watches the performance depicted as an ancient dance, the sight of which is hazy with incense or smoke from the burning of copal, a resin from a tree of the same name indigenous to Oaxaca, Mexico. Copal is often burned for ceremonial purposes. Alma enters a fugue state, suggesting that it rekindled something essential and primal deep within her. After the performance, one of the dancers is having a cigarette break outside and Alma joins her. They converse about what the performance stirred in Alma and the dancer asks, "And you're mestiza, right?" To which Alma replies that she is Mexican on her mother's side. The dancer rejoins, "Then it's in your blood." Here it can be inferred critically that a magical Indian makes her appearance to confirm Alma's indigeneity. I suggest that the Indian is pushed into the past, while the mestiza heralds a crip future in which she complexly weaves the different aspects of her identity together in complex ways that are not ascribed likewise to Indigenous peoples.

More in the vein of native studies and Indigenous theory, Juliana Hu Pegues's formulation of "space-time colonialism" brilliantly weaves together the fields of Indigenous studies and Asian American studies in ways that are helpful for the cross-racial, -temporal, and -linguist affinities in *Undone*.[34] Indigenous studies has critiqued the ways that settler time

**FIGURE 6** *Alma (right) with the "La Antigua" dancer, who wears a feathered, ceremonial headdress.*

has positioned Indigenous peoples outside of time either by relegating them to the past or rendering them non-modern subjects in the present. Meanwhile, Asian American studies has been more concerned, according to Hu Pegues, with the spatial (rather than specifically temporal) dynamics of racial capitalism, and the ways that these have prompted mass migration, labor exploitation, and community formation in the United States. Hu Pegues encourages the two fields to come together to think both time- and space-relationally, linking "the forever foreign and the never modern."[35] Where I believe Hu Pegues's analysis helps us in thinking about the multiple Borderlands of US territory and colonized spaces is in anchoring our understanding of settler colonialism vis-à-vis the production of the alien non-citizen in the form of either the racialized laborer, the assimilated/Americanized racial migrant, or even the temporally anachronistic Indian. Along with work by Iyko Day, Jodi A. Byrd, and Lisa Lowe, Hu Pegues demonstrates the ways that the racialized migrant is instrumentalized as a tool of racial capital, thereby changing space in order to facilitate its acquisition as white settler territory.[36] Settler territory thus implants a temporal colonial logic that positions native people outside of the time of the state—relegated to the past, destroyed, or inauthentically modern and, therefore, unable to possess or steward land.

## Conclusion

In this chapter I attempted to hone in on several interconnected issues in *Undone* in order to demonstrate the ways in which the show productively and innovatively threads together issues of disability and deafness, racial and immigrant identity, and cross-racial solidarity amongst Asian American and Latinx American subjects through the politics of language. This latter issue is particularly important, in that I suggest that a disability lens leads to and fundamentally enriches a comparative racial analysis in this case, thus bridging Native, Asian American, and Latinx studies. I contend that disability is fundamental for a comparative ethnic studies approach attentive to the formation of migrant subjectivities articulated in a relational web of racial-colonial histories. Similarly, how can disability studies better attend to the colonial frames of citizenship and settler colonialism in its vision for a more equitable society? These elements share particular grounded material realities that prompt migrations with varied historical ontologies to settler colonies like the United States. At the same time, however, the relational experience of incapacitation, disablement, and debility forges vital connections that are not always reducible to specific historical contexts. Disability is one of the mechanisms through which racial subjects are deemed not worthy citizens, while being a robust, fully-fledged citizen typically indicates a propertied relation to ability. The racialized ability of the citizen is often subsidized on the exploited capacities of the non-citizen alien. Rather than view race and disability as separate political issues, the historical and linguistic registers through which capacity and identity intersect become evident.

# CODA
## *Basement Archive in the Tropics*

I speak Tagalog with a Spanish accent. The synapses in my brain that accumulated Spanish knowledge braid and fray in the same cerebral space where Tagalog lives. The brain synaptically inflates like universes of mycelial tendrils that curl into each other, as do vines or veins. I reflect on the irony of using my brain to imagine itself. Like most US high-school students, I learned Spanish first. The first "foreign" language. Tagalog came later as an adult, with the help of US Department of Education funding. The mother tongue, English, feels more evenly and deeply dispersed throughout my neural tissue—entering and innervating cerebral plasticity in ways that signal what we commonly call native speech. Anglophone roots tangle with the nodes where I developed motor functions, depth perception, the ability to recognize faces, and the economy of involuntary life functions like breathing and peristalsis. My muscles contract with English grammar.

When I swallow, it is English.

When I am well rested with a homeostatic mood, it can be Spanish or Tagalog.

I have never cried in Tagalog.

My analytical mind and its ability to discern patterns—my waking consciousness—is where the languages I voluntarily learned reside. It is not where love lives. Nor fear. Nor hunger or passion. It is data. The dispassionate consumption of discrete units of information to form novel phrases that are merely the idea of creativity, rather than its actual materialization. This part of the mind is like a small apartment. A basement archive in the tropics. Crowded. Dank. Dimly lit with occasional blips of meager sunlight from a window with no southern exposure. Spanish and Tagalog do not seem to exist as separate bodies here. Rather, they act like a fluid plasma. Atoms in such a hot stew, they quantum tunnel into each other. Hydrogen becomes helium. These give way to boron and beryllium. And then even heavier elements come. My forehead smacks into a thud of iron where reactivity ceases. Hispanotagalog interferes with itself. I might say the very act of possessing Spanish ("my Spanish is pretty good") is its own defiant, self-defeating action. A closed system of linguistic colonization where the recognition I desire is the very misrecognition I despise and yet . . . love.

I say the Spanish words loaned to and repurposed by Tagalog like a Spaniard. So . . . correctly? "Lamesa," "Bintana," "Almusal," and "Cabalyo"—"the horse had lunch before leaping over the table through the window." What? Imagine being a Spanish person (of the language or the country) and you see yourself there, on the page, in an Austronesian language. Its ancestors' travels through archipelagos, the Indian Ocean, and the Pacific become *your* travels and *your* story somehow. Your Romance words like flags staked in the earth, dotting the horizon. My forked tongue is where the old world meets the new, only then to meet even older worlds. My mouth a tuning fork in spacetime. Sound becomes mass with a gravitational pull that folds space in on itself. It becomes a black hole without an event horizon. Its naked singularity a window into the future that is really the past.

As a Tagalog speaker, I st/utter and I feel like Madonna when she tries to fake a British accent. Or when Kendrick accuses Drake that he caught lingo in Atlanta to be more authentically hip hop. Peeling away to Manila, I feel uneasy as my bronzed Filipino face (I did not fear the sun) strode the sidewalks of Katipunan Avenue squawking with the voice of a Spanish exchange student, my vocal chords betraying me. I felt "sosyal," a Spanish or US English loanword connoting snobbery or unearned elegance.

Though when I speak my mongrel Spanish-Tagalog, I kind of love it. It is me and not me somehow.

A queer ilustrado with a brain like a special vessel for strange truths and fermented fruits. To speak is to bare teeth cut on the folds of history.

With knives I clamp my jaw closed.

My mind commands my face to present a countenance that others can comprehend.

I conform myself to recognition as a function of the misreading of others.

A manila galleon plunking clumsily on the ocean floor.

Dark pacific waters suck up the sunlight that might reflect off of it.

## On the Poetics of Misrecognition

Misrecognition is painful. Sometimes unbearable. However, that pain indicates a poetics of intersubjective being. It summons what Cassius Adair has called "the misrecognition you can bear," meaning, in this context, that it is an allusion that co-implicates us in communities and histories that we ought not have been estranged from in the first place. Drawing on Lauren Berlant's stunning observation that all recognition is misrecognition—"recognition is the misrecognition you can bear"—Adair highlights the fundamental instability of coalescing one's gender via the violent bureaucracies of state. While the unraveling and the re-congealing of one's gender is not something I underestimate, I think that racial misrecognition takes on a different character in its various comminglings with and as racialized gender. Whereas there exist, to my mind, ample political reasons to de-prioritize a propertied relation to gender—for instance, I am not protective over a (normative) masculinity I just happened to be born into—the ethical horizons of taking up and situating one's body within the racial affects and meanings that historically pertain to another are more controversial.

I have suggested that the aesthetic and political meanings of the brown Filipinx body point toward its power as metonymy. What does it mean when your brown body metonymizes history, geography, and community not quite your own? And what could it mean if such misrecognitions inform the structure of your very being and self-understanding—when the not you is also you, or a version thereof? That is to say, might there be a "lean in" possibility with misrecognition that does not devolve into masquerade? Where the concerns of others can become, fundamentally, your concerns, but where the possessive pronoun indexes a non-propertied relation to identity? Where identification *with* takes prominence over identification *as*? I believe that the uncanny quality of misrecognition actually reveals more than we could claim that it obscures. The misrecognitive, for me, has aided in fleshing out a cartography of kin that suspends the fetish of ethnonational narrowness, thus supplanting such with a more imaginative and organic relational kinship materially defined by the actual migratory moves of history. *Dos X* has argued that these migratory historical moves are imbued within that moment of mis/recognition. Thus, misrecognition exists as a sort of relational archive *en carne viva*, rather than what we imagine to be bounded historical archives where official categorization or recognition may reign.

I hesitate to affirm that, in this way, the Filipina/o can be misrecognitively Latina/o.

As a young and green professor in Tucson, I began my career teaching a predominantly working-class and Mexican American student body. For instance, in a Spanish literary survey I taught, of the twenty-five students, twenty-three identified as Mexican or Mexican American. Some even crossed the border weekly to attend the class (the university was approximately ninety miles from the US-Mexico border). It was a joy for me to be in this environment, with students for whom the study of Spanish was inescapably connected to the Borderlands politics of where we were situated.

Often the pedagogical encounter reveals deep truths about epistemic authority and identity that are hard to avoid. I have written in other contexts on what it might mean to be a Filipino professor of Spanish in a US context. During those sweltering months in Tucson, I insisted that the Spanish language canon that I surveyed include Chicano/a politics and history. I imagined that this would resonate with the largely Mexican class I had before me. To my surprise, "Chicano" was seen by most of the students as a downgrade—a subclass of Mexican existence subordinate to real Mexican identity. I respected that many of the students were not simply Mexican American as second or third generation subjects. Mexican American identity, in the truest and most challenging sense, was an itinerant formation living hither and thither. Many of my students were consistent border crossers, with family often in Yuma and Tucson, and they thus existed in a Mexican America that was animate, active, and constantly under definition. It was not a staid historical fact that fit in the genealogical strictures of a literary survey. I felt out of my depth as the presumptive authority giving language to their experiences.

It felt colonial.

What do I mean by this? I mean it was colonialism that cleaved their experiences into two national spaces. It was colonialism that obstructed their kinship networks with border checkpoints, often staffed by relatives enacting the oppressive laws of state. And it was colonialism that established the hierarchical pedagogical scene in which I assumed epistemic authority to impose an expertise, however respectfully and carefully, on the mosaic of their lives. And yet, it was also colonialism that displaced and arranged us into a novel kinship pattern of relationality, where the Filipino professor of Spanish could potentially be an ethical figure of solidarity—at least, I hoped.

It was this arrangement, in the deserts of Sonoma, wherein I first began to think about the ethical relationalities inherent to misrecognition—the play and theoretical gravitas that errors of recognition could highlight invisibilized historical encounters dispersed by the knowledge systems of coloniality. Moreover, misrecognition as a form of ethical encounter with an other could set the stage for the coauthorship of different ethical and identitarian relationalities that *exceed* colonial epistemologies.

When I brought up "Chicano studies" and "Chicana/o identity" to my Borderlands students, they seemed like historical artifacts. Maybe a deranged labor activist uncle would reminisce about times past in ways that annoyed rather than edified. "Chicano" was representative of a stunted recognition of try-hards that were angry at their foreclosed access to true Mexicanness. Why be Chicano when you could be *mexicano*? In some ways, coming to such a conclusion is quite reasonable. When confronted with texts that at times confront the malaise of misrecognition produced through a perceived distance or even exile from Mexico, why not orient yourself toward the lost object of Mexicanness disarticulated from you? Is such a return not a source of true agency? Why not gleefully and proudly identify as mexicano, particularly in a borderized environment that was unambiguously a part of Mexico and, in many ways, persists as a part of Mexico, where people, customs, and tradition are concerned?

I slowly started to make a case for Chicana/o politics as a vital historical advent of migrant labor mobilization that would be obfuscated by too seamless a political attachment to the Mexican or US nation-states. It was farmworkers that lived on the border between the two, and whose material conditions of survivance and imposed stoop-labor slow death engineered a unique political subjectivity unreducible to the hegemonic nation form.

I was the Filipino defending the Chicano and engendering suspicion in political bonds to Mexico as the only horizon of political possibility.

But in making this defense, I was also making a defense of Filipino American politics.

The United Farm Workers movement was a historical event that tied Filipino American and Mexican American politics together in a way that would have been invisibilized if "Chicano" was swept to the dustbin of obsolescence. The encounter between Larry Itliong, César Chávez, and Dolores Huerta would be misrecognized and effaced if we do not attune ourselves to the interstices that compose binational political economies. It was Filipino workers initially going on strike that prompted a multiracial labor movement that tied the destinies of multiple communities across language, race, and geography. I conveyed that the Philippines and Filipino America do not necessarily exist in México, but do and did surface in Mexican America.

Pursuing a move to integrate Filipinx studies with Latinx studies, I thought about the genre of this very conclusion as a kind of coda. As defined in *Merriam-Webster*'s, a coda is "1. a concluding part of a literary or dramatic work. 2. something that serves to round out, conclude, or summarize and usually has its own interest." An additional intriguing definition positions the coda as "a concluding musical section that is formally distinct from the main structure." In other words, an addition that "has its own interest" and is "formally distinct" from the main substance. I wonder if we might think of Filipinx studies as a kind of "coda" for Latinx studies, or Filipinx people as existing in a kind of filial relation with Latinx American people, but as also and still "distinct from the main structure." We saw this in the case of Jose Antonio Vargas (recall Jose without an accent, as he made it formally known). He sought to open up the immigration debate in the United States so that its racial and national terms could be more inclusive. Though such distinctiveness seems to meet its limits in novels like Brian Ascalon Roley's *American Son*, in which Filipino American characters desire to re-present themselves as Mexican American. I argued that this enabled different kinds of economic exchanges in the racial economy of southern California and offered horizontal alternatives to vertical assimilation into white normativity. Such potentiality for misrecognition is partly enabled by the placement of Filipinos within a brown mestizo archive. In my first book, *Crip Colony*, I made the case for the importance of a Filipino archive of mestizaje in literary and historical work that was in dialogue with but also independent from other mestizaje projects across the American republics. However, in *Dos X*, I have been less concerned about the boundedness of the nation-state in delineating the borders of national projects. In the diaspora, such boundedness can be vexed completely, thus building something new in the new homeland often in multiracial coalition and in dialogue with others displaced or replaced by the vicissitudes of American imperialisms.

In reflecting on the moment of misrecognition, I began this book remarking on a dysphoric feeling. I now end it with that same feeling. Dysphoria prompts translation of language and translation through space. In the introduction, I reflected on how misrecognition of my person put me in a different ethical and subjective relation to the migratory and racial histories of my immediate environment. This carried me to Tucson, as I have related above. It was the misrecognitive that set my sights and intellectual interests on the Spanish language—an orientation that was and continues to be, ironically, a product of a racial error. Can there be a kind of racial drag without the masquerade? Can the synecdoche of self collapse the racial estrangements conjured by misrecognition? Can there be a collapse that ushers one away from the liberal antinomies of representation and thus moves one to a different kind of ethical subjecthood productively oriented *toward* the disfigurements wrought by capital?

Acknowledgments

I would like to thank all my students past and present. Their dialogue and generosity were instrumental in completing this book. I would also like to thank all my colleagues in the Department of Spanish and Latinx and Latin American studies at Amherst College. Their support for my, at times, idiosyncratic thinking has always been appreciated. These departments represent fields that have many very good reasons to be geographically conservative, but my colleagues have embraced the radical potential of differing histories, pedagogies, and perspectives that traverse a much broader "Hispanic" world. I often found myself encouraged and even emboldened by their enthusiasm when I felt demotivated. Thank you to Alicia, Daniela, Ilán, Leah, Lloyd, Ludmila, Paul, Rick, Russ, Sara, Sarah, and Solsiree.

Over the years, I have relied on the intellectual camaraderie of the "boy luck club"—a writing retreat for queer Asian American professors. A lifeline in times of dread and ennui, I continue to rely on Ian, James, Kareem, Matthew, James, and Tom. This group, if my count is correct, has written ten books in each other's company. Writing really can be world and community building.

I wanted to spare a moment to give a special thanks to three individuals whose thinking and writing have made a profound impact and difference on what I have theorized in this book. Ava Kim has spent countless hours workshopping ideas and thinking with me through an expansive archive of mestizaje which started, for me, with my first book project. She is a courageous thinker who bravely traverses language and continent to pursue justice for transgender people. I also wish to thank Cassius Adair, whose own theories on misrecognition and state power have indelibly shaped my own thinking on these topics. I am thankful that such a prominent trans theorist approached me with a lot of compassion and open-mindedness with my first-draft-thinking on racial dysphoria. This book might not be better than that first draft outline, but those errors reside with me. And finally, I want to thank stef torralba, with whom I spent many hours discussing the intersection of Latinx and Filipinx cultural politics. It is rare to find such a gifted interlocutor whose unimpeachable quality of mind sheds new light on things you have thought about for a very long time.

I also extend my gratitude to the University of Minnesota Press, the journal *Critical Ethnic Studies* and its editors, for permission to include an adapted version of the article "Manifest Disablement: Cripping the Frontier Thesis of American History" (8.1, Spring 2023) as a chapter in *Dos X*. The review process for this article and the various forms of reviewer and editorial feedback were instrumental in the formation of my thinking toward what would become this book.

# Notes

## Introduction

1. Octavio Paz, *El Laberinto de La Soledad*, Letras Hispánicas (Cátedra, 1993), 346.
2. Paula C. Park, "Transpacific Intercoloniality: Rethinking the Globality of Philippine Literature in Spanish," *Journal of Spanish Cultural Studies* 20, nos. 1–2 (March 2019): 83–97. https://doi.org/10.1080/14636204.2019.1609236.
3. Lennard J. Davis, "Constructing Normalcy: The Bell Curve, the Novel, and the Invention of the Disabled Body in the Nineteenth Century," in *The Disability Studies Reader*, ed. Lennard J. Davis (New York: Routledge, 1997), 9–28.
4. Beth Lew-Williams, *The Chinese Must Go: Violence, Exclusion, and the Making of the Alien in America* (Cambridge: Harvard University Press, 2018); Lisa Lowe, *Immigrant Acts: On Asian American Cultural Politics* (Durham: Duke University Press, 1996); Iyko Day, *Alien Capital: Asian Racialization and the Logic of Settler Colonial Capitalism* (Durham: Duke University Press, 2016); Denise Ferreira da Silva, *Toward a Global Idea of Race*, Borderlines 27 (Minneapolis: University of Minnesota Press, 2007); Mae M. Ngai, *Impossible Subjects: Illegal Aliens and the Making of Modern America* (Princeton: Princeton University Press, 2004); Ronald T. Takaki, *Strangers from a Different Shore: A History of Asian Americans*, rev. ed. (Boston: Little, Brown and Company, 1998); Nayan Shah, *Stranger Intimacy: Contesting Race, Sexuality, and the Law in the North American West*, American Crossroads 31 (Berkeley: University of California Press, 2011).
5. Julie Avril Minich, *Accessible Citizenships: Disability, Nation, and the Cultural Politics of Greater Mexico* (Philadelphia: Temple University Press, 2014).
6. Douglas C. Baynton, *Defectives in the Land: Disability and Immigration in the Age of Eugenics* (Chicago: University of Chicago Press, 2016); Margot Canaday, *The Straight State: Sexuality and Citizenship in Twentieth-Century America*, Politics and Society in Twentieth-Century America (Princeton: Princeton University Press, 2009); Paul K. Longmore and Lauri Umansky, *The New Disability History: American Perspectives*, The History of Disability (New York: New

York University Press, 2001); Kim E. Nielsen, *A Disability History of the United States*, ReVisioning American History (Boston: Beacon Press, 2012); Nayan Shah, *Contagious Divides: Epidemics and Race in San Francisco's Chinatown*, American Crossroads 7 (Berkeley: University of California Press, 2001).

7. Shah, *Contagious Divides*.
8. Susan Burch, *Committed: Remembering Native Kinship in and beyond Institutions*, Critical Indigeneities (Chapel Hill: University of North Carolina Press, 2021); Jessica Cowing, "Settler States of Ability: Assimilation, Incarceration, and Native Women's Crip Interventions" (PhD diss., William & Mary, 2020). http://dx.doi.org/10.21220/s2-j31a-n741.
9. Cowing, "Settler States of Ability."
10. Sarita See, "Southern Postcoloniality and the Improbability of Filipino-American Postcoloniality," *Mississippi Quarterly* 57, no. 1 (Winter 2003–2004): 41–54; Victor Román Mendoza, "A Queer Nomadology of Jessica Hagedorn's *Dogeaters*," *American Literature: A Journal of Literary History, Criticism, and Bibliography* 77, no. 4 (December 12, 2005): 815–845. See also Jessica Hagedorn, *Dogeaters* (New York: Penguin Books, 1991).
11. Alicia Arrizón, *Queering Mestizaje: Transculturation and Performance*, Triangulations (Ann Arbor: University of Michigan Press, 2006); Rudy P. Guevarra, Jr., *Becoming Mexipino: Multiethnic Identities and Communities in San Diego*, Latinidad: Transnational Cultures in the United States (New Brunswick: Rutgers University Press, 2012); Allan Punzalan Isaac, *American Tropics: Articulating Filipino America*, Critical American Studies (Minneapolis: University of Minnesota Press, 2006); Long Le-Khac, *Giving Form to an Asian and Latinx America*, Stanford Studies in Comparative Race and Ethnicity (Stanford University Press, 2020); Anthony Christian Ocampo, *The Latinos of Asia: How Filipino Americans Break the Rules of Race* (Stanford: Stanford University Press, 2016); Sony Coráñez Bolton, *Crip Colony: Mestizaje, US Imperialism, and the Queer Politics of Disability in the Philippines* (Durham: Duke University Press, 2023).
12. Martin Joseph Ponce, *Beyond the Nation: Diasporic Filipino Literature and Queer Reading*, Sexual Cultures (New York: New York University Press, 2012).
13. See the foundational Judith Butler, *Gender Trouble: Feminism and the Subversion of Identity* (New York: Routledge, 1999).
14. Cassius Adair, "Is Transsexualism Chronic?" *Feminist Studies* 48, no. 2 (2022): 475–501. https://doi.org/10.1353/fem.2022.0036.
15. Coráñez Bolton, *Crip Colony*.
16. Philip Joseph Deloria, *Playing Indian* (New Haven: Yale University Press, 1998).
17. News Forum, "'Pretendians': Why Are People Pretending to Be Indigenous?" February 21, 2023. https://www.youtube.com/watch?v=_Ozv5bd7gCo.
18. Adrienne Keene, "A Letter to Elizabeth Hoover," *Native Appropriations*, May 2, 2023. https://nativeappropriations.com/2023/05/a-letter-to-elizabeth-hoover.html.

19. Keene, "Letter to Hoover."
20. Keene, "Letter to Hoover."
21. Sony Coráñez Bolton, "A Tale of Two 'X's: Queer Filipinx and Latinx Linguistic Intimacies," in *Filipinx American Studies: Reckoning, Reclamation, Transformation*, ed. Rick Bonus and Antonio T. Tiongson (New York: Fordham University Press, 2022), 284–290. https://doi.org/10.2307/j.ctv2gmhh8s.28.
22. Georg Wilhelm Fredrich Hegel, *The Phenomenology of Spirit*, ed. Terry Pinkard and Michael Baur (Cambridge: Cambridge University Press, 2018). https://doi.org/10.1017/9781139050494.
23. Hegel, "Lordship and Bondage," in *The Phenomenology of Spirit*, 109.
24. W. E. B. Du Bois and Jonathan Scott Holloway, *The Souls of Black Folk* (New Haven: Yale University Press, 2015).
25. Emmanuel Levinas, *Totality and Infinity: An Essay on Exteriority* (Leiden: Martinus Nijhoff Publishers, 1979).
26. David T. Mitchell and Sharon L. Snyder, *Narrative Prosthesis: Disability and the Dependencies of Discourse*, Corporealities (Ann Arbor: University of Michigan Press, 2000).

## Chapter 1: Ability as Property

1. Iyko Day, "Being or Nothingness: Indigeneity, Antiblackness, and Settler Colonial Critique," *Critical Ethnic Studies* 1, no. 2 (2015): 102–121. https://doi.org/10.5749/jcritethnstud.1.2.0102; Cheryl I. Harris, "Whiteness as Property," *Harvard Law Review* 106, no. 8 (1993): 1707–1791. https://doi.org/10.2307/1341787; Lisa Lowe, *The Intimacies of Four Continents* (Durham: Duke University Press, 2015); Denise Ferreira da Silva, *Toward a Global Idea of Race*, Borderlines 27 (Minneapolis: University of Minnesota Press, 2007).
2. Harris, "Whiteness"; David Lloyd, "Race under Representation." *Oxford Literary Review* 13, nos. 1–2 (1991): 62–94.
3. Martha Craven Nussbaum, *Creating Capabilities: The Human Development Approach* (London: Harvard University Press, 2011); Stacy Clifford Simplican, *The Capacity Contract: Intellectual Disability and the Question of Citizenship* (Minneapolis & London: University of Minnesota Press, 2015).
4. George Lipsitz, *The Possessive Investment in Whiteness: How White People Profit from Identity Politics*, 20th anniversary ed. (Philadelphia: Temple University Press, 2018).
5. Frederick Jackson Turner, *The Significance of the Frontier in American History*, Proceedings of the Forty-First Annual Meeting of the State Historical Society of Wisconsin (Madison: State Historical Society of Wisconsin, 1894).
6. For an analysis on how these logics manifest in the American imperial museum, see Sarita Echavez, *The Filipino Primitive: Accumulation and Resistance in the American Museum* (New York: New York University Press, 2017).

7. William McKinley, "Benevolent Assimilation," memorandum to the US Secretary of War, December 21, 1898 (2016); Stuart Creighton Miller, *"Benevolent Assimilation": The American Conquest of the Philippines, 1899–1903* (New Haven: Yale University Press, 1982).
8. Frederick Jackson Turner, with commentary and edited by John Mack Faragher, *Rereading Frederick Jackson Turner: "The Significance of the Frontier in American History" and Other Essays* (New Haven: Yale University Press, 1998).
9. Much of my thought on "transpacific" critique is derived from Asian Americanist scholars of the Cold War Pacific. While it is not the central aim of this chapter, I am suggesting that the American frontier at the end of the nineteenth century was an epochal moment in the global US orientation toward the Pacific, which cannot be completely explained by the Cold War. For more on this phenomenon, see Isaac, *American Tropics*; Lisa Yoneyama, *Cold War Ruins: Transpacific Critique of American Justice and Japanese War Crimes* (Durham: Duke University Press, 2016); Jodi Kim, *Ends of Empire: Asian American Critique and the Cold War*, Critical American Studies (Minneapolis: University of Minnesota Press, 2010).
10. Eunjung Kim, *Curative Violence: Rehabilitating Disability, Gender, and Sexuality in Modern Korea* (Durham: Duke University Press, 2017).
11. I take the idea of an "archive of liberalism" from Lowe's *The Intimacies of Four Continents*.
12. For the original coining of the term "crip-of-color critique," see Jina B. Kim, "Toward a Crip-of-Color Critique: Thinking with Minich's 'Enabling Whom?'" *Lateral* 6, no. 1 (Spring 2017). http://csalateral.org/issue/6-1/forum-alt-humanities-critical-disability-studies-crip-of-color-critique-kim. More recently, Kim and Schalk have extended thinking on this concept in Jina B. Kim and Sami Schalk, "Reclaiming the Radical Politics of Self-Care: A Crip-of-Color Critique," *South Atlantic Quarterly* 120, no. 2 (April 4, 2021): 325–342. https://doi.org/10.1215/00382876-8916074. For further reading on the racial politics of disability, see Minich, *Accessible Citizenships*; Sami Schalk, *Bodyminds Reimagined: (Dis)Ability, Race, and Gender in Black Women's Speculative Fiction* (Durham & London: Duke University Press, 2018).
13. Jasbir K. Puar, *The Right to Maim: Debility, Capacity, Disability*, Anima (Durham: Duke University Press, 2017).
14. Mike Oliver, "The Social Model of Disability: Thirty Years On," *Disability & Society* 28, no. 7 (2013): 1024–1026.
15. Chris Bell, "Introducing White Disability Studies: A Modest Proposal," in *The Disability Studies Reader*, ed. Lennard J. Davis, 2nd ed. (New York: Routledge, 2006), 275–282; Nirmala Erevelles, *Disability and Difference in Global Contexts: Enabling a Transformative Body Politic* (London: Palgrave Macmillan, 2011); Clare Barker and Stuart Murray, "Disabling Postcolonialism: Global Disability Cultures and Democratic Criticism," *Journal of Literary & Cultural*

*Disability Studies* 4, no. 3 (2010): 219–236; Sony Coráñez Bolton, "Cripping the Philippine Enlightenment: Ilustrado Travel Literature, Postcolonial Disability, and the 'Normate Imperial Eye/I,'" *Verge: Studies in Global Asias* 2, no. 2 (2016): 138–162. https://doi.org/10.5749/vergstudglobasia.2.2.0138.

16. For more on the concept and theorizations of epistemic violence, see Gayatri Chakravorty Spivak, *Can the Subaltern Speak?: Reflections on the History of an Idea*, ed. Rosalind C. Morris (New York: Columbia University Press, 2010); Gayatri Chakravorty Spivak, *A Critique of Postcolonial Reason: Toward a History of the Vanishing Present* (Cambridge: Harvard University Press, 1999).
17. Lowe, *The Intimacies of Four Continents*; Simplican, *The Capacity Contract*; Nussbaum, *Creating Capabilities*.
18. Lee D. Baker, *From Savage to Negro: Anthropology and the Construction of Race, 1896–1954* (Berkeley: University of California Press, 1998).
19. One Peruvian sociologist called this "coloniality." See Aníbal Quijano and Michael Ennis, "Coloniality of Power, Eurocentrism, and Latin America," *Nepantla: Views from South* 1, no. 3 (2000): 533–581.
20. Ato Quayson, *Aesthetic Nervousness: Disability and the Crisis of Representation* (New York: Columbia University Press, 2007).
21. Robert McRuer, *Crip Theory: Cultural Signs of Queerness and Disability*, Cultural Front (New York: New York University Press, 2006).
22. McRuer, *Crip Theory*; Alison Kafer, *Feminist, Queer, Crip* (Bloomington: Indiana University Press, 2013); Tobin Siebers, *Disability Theory* (Ann Arbor: University of Michigan Press, 2008); David T. Mitchell and Sharon L. Snyder, *The Biopolitics of Disability: Neoliberalism, Ablenationalism, and Peripheral Embodiment*, Corporealities (Ann Arbor: University of Michigan Press, 2015); Rosemarie Garland-Thomson, *Extraordinary Bodies: Figuring Physical Disability in American Culture and Literature* (New York: Columbia University Press, 2017); Minich, *Accessible Citizenships*.
23. Crip theorist Lennard J. Davis has captured this anxiety around disability and impairment in his concept "dismodernism." See Lennard J. Davis, *Bending over Backwards: Disability, Dismodernism, and Other Difficult Positions*, Cultural Front (New York: New York University Press, 2002).
24. Mitchell and Snyder, *Narrative Prosthesis*.
25. Margaret Price, "The Bodymind Problem and the Possibilities of Pain," *Hypatia: A Journal of Feminist Philosophy* 30, no. 1 (2015): 268–284.
26. Of course, this dispossession of non-white bodies functions neither uniformly nor monolithically for all racialized groups.
27. Robert McRuer and Michael Berube, *Introduction: Compulsory Able-Bodiedness and Queer/Disabled Existence* (New York: New York University Press, 2006).
28. David Harvey, *The New Imperialism* (Oxford & New York: Oxford University Press, 2005).
29. Harris, "Whiteness," 1714.

30. Harris, "Whiteness," 1716.
31. Here, "property" has the dual meaning of economic "good" and of a trait, both of which are things that one can "possess."
32. Harris, "Whiteness," 1720.
33. Harris, "Whiteness," 1721.
34. Harris, "Whiteness," 1721.
35. Day, "Being or Nothingness."
36. Patrick Wolfe, "Recuperating Binarism: A Heretical Introduction," *Settler Colonial Studies* 3, nos. 3–4 (2013): 257–279.
37. Tiya Miles, *Ties That Bind: The Story of an Afro-Cherokee Family in Slavery and Freedom*, 2nd ed., American Crossroads 14 (Berkeley: University of California Press, 2015). Miles explores the case of a Cherokee Indian possessing Black slaves.
38. Sylvia Wynter, "Unsettling the Coloniality of Being/Power/Truth/Freedom: Towards the Human, After Man, Its Overrepresentation—An Argument," *CR: The New Centennial Review* 3, no. 3 (2003): 257–337. https://doi.org/10.1353/ncr.2004.0015; Quijano and Ennis, "Coloniality of Power," 533; Fernando Ortiz and Harriet de Onis, *Cuban Counterpoint: Tobacco and Sugar* (New York: Vintage Books, 1970).
39. Harris, "Whiteness," 1726, 1727–1728.
40. Harris, "Whiteness," 1728.
41. Turner, *The Significance of the Frontier*, 2.
42. Turner, *The Significance of the Frontier*, 2.
43. Mitchell and Snyder, *Narrative Prosthesis*, 7.
44. Mitchell and Snyder, *Narrative Prosthesis*, 6.
45. Mitchell and Snyder, *Narrative Prosthesis*, 8.
46. Patrick Wolfe, "Settler colonialism and the elimination of the native," *Journal of Genocide Research* 8, no. 4 (2006): 387–409.
47. Wolfe, "Settler colonialism," 389.
48. María Josefina Saldaña-Portillo, *Indian Given: Racial Geographies across Mexico and the United States*, Latin America Otherwise (Durham: Duke University Press, 2016).
49. Turner and Faragher, *Rereading Frederick Jackson Turner*, 31–60.
50. Siebers, *Disability Theory*, 8.
51. Siebers, *Disability Theory*, 8.
52. Turner, *The Significance of the Frontier,* 48.
53. Turner, *The Significance of the Frontier*, 33.
54. I take the language of rupture to be delineated in transnational feminist critique. See Grace Kyungwon Hong, *The Ruptures of American Capital: Women of Color Feminism and the Culture of Immigrant Labor* (Minneapolis: University of Minnesota Press, 2006).
55. Amy Kaplan, "Manifest Domesticity," *American Literature* 70, no. 3 (1998): 581–606. https://doi.org/10.2307/2902710.

56. My use of the term "normate" comes from Garland-Thomson, *Extraordinary Bodies*. In Garland-Thomson's novel intervention, she theorizes the normate as a particular kind of normative embodiment shaped through ableism.
57. Kaplan, "Manifest Domesticity," 583.
58. Kaplan, "Manifest Domesticity," 587.
59. Turner, *The Significance of the Frontier*, 44–45.
60. Roderick A. Ferguson, *Aberrations in Black: Toward a Queer of Color Critique* (Minneapolis: University of Minnesota Press, 2004).
61. Ferguson, *Aberrations in Black*, 2–3. The quotation from Reddy is taken from Chandan Reddy, "Home, Houses, Nonidentity: 'Paris Is Burning,'" in *Burning Down the House: Recycling Domesticity*, ed. Rosemary Marangoly George (Boulder: Westview Press, 1997), 356–357.
62. Ferguson, *Aberrations in Black*, 18.
63. Ferguson, *Aberrations in Black*, 6.
64. Ferguson, *Aberrations in Black*, 6. Emphasis in original.
65. Karl Marx, *Capital: A Critique of Political Economy. The Process of Capitalist Production*, trans. Eden Paul and Cedar Paul (London: Allen & Unwin, 1928).
66. Scott Lauria Morgensen, "Settler Homonationalism: Theorizing Settler Colonialism within Queer Modernities," *GLQ: A Journal of Lesbian and Gay Studies* 16, no. 1 (2010): 105–131.
67. Mark Rifkin, *When Did Indians Become Straight?: Kinship, the History of Sexuality, and Native Sovereignty* (Oxford: Oxford University Press, 2011).
68. Turner, *The Significance of the Frontier*, 32.
69. Kaplan, "Manifest Domesticity," 588.
70. David Lloyd, "Race under Representation," *Oxford Literary Review* 13, nos. 1–2 (1991): 62–94. I take from Lloyd the phrase "subject without properties," by which he means an unmarked white male subject as the unspoken universal center of history and theory. They are "without properties" because their universality is taken for granted. Other subjects are more peripheral because they unmistakably have the property of "race."
71. Gail Bederman, *Manliness & Civilization: A Cultural History of Gender and Race in the United States, 1880–1917*, Women in Culture and Society (Chicago: University of Chicago Press, 1995).
72. Turner, *The Significance of the Frontier*, 31.
73. Bederman, *Manliness & Civilization*; Kristin L. Hoganson, *Fighting for American Manhood: How Gender Politics Provoked the Spanish-American and Philippine-American Wars*, Yale Historical Publications (New Haven: Yale University Press, 1998); Victor Román Mendoza, *Metroimperial Intimacies: Fantasy, Racial-Sexual Governance, and the Philippines in U.S. Imperialism, 1899–1913*, Perverse Modernities (Durham: Duke University Press, 2015).
74. Kafer, *Feminist, Queer, Crip*.

## Chapter 2: Filipinx Spanish

1. I wrote about this topic extensively in my first book, *Crip Colony*.
2. Here I refer to Octavio Paz's *El Laberinto de la soledad*, a foundational text in Mexican enlightenment discourse, which includes an unexpected (perhaps) critique of the artifice of Chicano identity in the form of the pachuco. While not invoked in the current analysis, Paz's misogynistic appraisals of Mexican femininity and the perverse effeminacy of US Chicano subjectivity as immanently penetrate-able have inspired my transnational take on the repetition of Philippine Enlightenment discourse as racial project in Filipino American cultural forms. What *American Son* labels as "Asian and Spanish heritage" functionalizes intellectual patrimony as racial inheritance of mestizo characteristics. The paradigmatic embodiment of enlightened patrimony as racial type is, of course, José Rizal, the Chinese-mestizo hacendado intellectual luminary of Philippine nationalist historiography. His racial aesthetics, indeed, underwrite much of the current analysis.
3. Such linguistic capacities and incapacities highlight a constellation of social and historical forces that have come to shape Filipino understandings of colonial, archival, and political filiations as, at once, Hispanic, Asian, Asian American, and American. In highlighting the status of Filipinos as not Hispanophone, as a caveat, I will not endorse that Filipinos should learn Spanish in order to truly access their histories, for this minimizes the colonial technologies that affected the linguistic colonialism in the Philippines. I locate the absence of Spanish through a non-deficit-based analysis drawing on disability theory. Indeed, it is through disability theory that we can begin to approach the incapacity to speak the language through which colonial governance guided the racialization, Christianization, and colonization of the Philippines not as a lack, in the deficit-based sense of the word, but, rather, as an opportunity for crucial comparative work between the transpacific borderscape of the Philippines and the US-Mexican corridor. Linguistic incapacity also signals a comparative framing wherein I intentionally connect Chicana feminist theory to Filipino American studies.
4. See Baynton, *Defectives in the land*; Nussbaum, *Creating Capabilities*; Davis, "Constructing Normalcy"; Canaday, *The Straight State*.
5. Ruben Zecena, "Migrating Like a Queen: Visuality and Performance in the Trans Gay Caravan," *WSQ: Women's Studies Quarterly* 47, no. 3 (2019): 99–118. https://doi.org/10.1353/wsq.2019.0063.
6. Mendoza, "A Queer Nomadology."
7. Xiomara Verenice Cervantes-Gómez has offered a fruitful critique of Octavio Paz's homophobia. See Xiomara Verenice Cervantes-Gómez, "Paz's Pasivo: Thinking Mexicanness from the Bottom," *Journal of Latin American Cultural Studies* 29, no. 3 (July 2020): 333–347. https://doi.org/10.1080/13569325.2019.1675146.
8. Cameron Awkward-Rich, *The Terrible We: Thinking with Trans Maladjustment* (Durham: Duke University Press, 2022); Cassius Adair, "Is Transsexualism

Chronic?" https://doi.org/10.1353/fem.2022.0036; Kadji Amin, "We Are All Nonbinary: A Brief History of Accidents," *Representations* 158, no. 1 (May 2022): 106–119. https://doi.org/10.1525/rep.2022.158.11.106; Susan Stryker, "{We Who Are Sexy}: Christine Jorgensen's Transsexual Whiteness in the Postcolonial Philippines," *Social Semiotics* 19, no. 1 (March 2009): 79–91.

9. C. Riley Snorton, *Black on Both Sides: A Racial History of Trans Identity* (Minneapolis: University of Minnesota Press, 2017).
10. Sora Han's work on the legal emergence of an Asian American subject as paradigmatically antiblack is instructive here. See especially Sora Han, "The Politics of Race in Asian American Jurisprudence," *UCLA Asian Pacific American Law Journal* 11 (Spring 2006): 1–40.
11. Gloria Anzaldúa, *Borderlands: The New Mestiza = La Frontera* (San Francisco: Aunt Lute Books, 2012).
12. Lonnie Carter, *The Romance of Magno Rubio* (New York: Broadway Play Publishing, 2005), 4–5.
13. Lowe, *Immigrant Acts*.
14. Simplican, *The Capacity Contract*.
15. Anzaldúa, *Borderlands*.
16. I suggest that it is through the absent presence of Spanish, rather than its affirmative articulation, where we can imagine comparative work for populations that have historical experience of Spanish and US imperialisms. To be clear, it is the linguistic inability of Filipinos to speak Spanish that I wish to focus upon in order to think through comparative colonial racialization.
17. Carlos Bulosan, "The Romance of Magno Rubio," in *Fiction by Filipinos in America*, ed. Cecilia Manguerra Brainard (Quezon City: New Day Publishers, 1993), 79.
18. Isaac, *American Tropics*, 2.
19. For more about this period in Philippine Hispanic history, see Teodoro A. Agoncillo, "Philippine Historiography in the Age of Kalaw," *Solidarity* 5 (January 1, 1984): 3–16; Paul Kramer, *The Blood of Government: Race, Empire, the United States and the Philippines* (Chapel Hill: University of North Carolina Press, 2006); Benedict R. O'G. Anderson, *Imagined Communities: Reflections on the Origin and Spread of Nationalism* (London: Verso, 2016); Raquel A. G. Reyes, *Love, Passion and Patriotism: Sexuality and the Philippine Propaganda Movement, 1882–1892*, Critical Dialogues in Southeast Asian Studies (Singapore & Seattle: NUS Press, in association with University of Washington Press, 2008).
20. Isaac, *American Tropics*, 178.
21. Isaac, *American Tropics*, 178–179.
22. Martin Manalansan, *Global Divas: Filipino Gay Men in the Diaspora* (Durham: Duke University Press, 2003), 180.
23. Roderick Ferguson, *The Reorder of Things: The University and Its Pedagogies of Minority Difference* (Minneapolis: University of Minnesota Press, 2012). Jodi

Melamed, *Represent and Destroy: Rationalizing Violence in the New Racial Capitalism* (Minneapolis: University of Minnesota Press, 2011); Chandan Reddy, *Freedom with Violence: Race, Sexuality and the US State* (Durham: Duke University Press, 2011).

24. For critical takes on the US regulations of race and sexuality through marriage, see Siobhan Somerville, *Queering the Color Line: Race and the Invention of Homosexuality in American Culture* (Durham: Duke University Press, 2000), and her article on miscegenation statutes, "Queer Loving," *GLQ: A Journal of Lesbian and Gay Studies* 11, no. 3 (2005): 335–370.
25. Sarita See, "Gambling with Debt: Lessons from the Illiterate," *American Quarterly* 64. no. 3 (September 2012): 495–513.
26. See, "Gambling with Debt."
27. Simplican, *The Capacity Contract.*
28. There is a robust bibliography on the ways in which race indexes both economic and intellectual debility. See "Accumulation, Dispossession, and Debt: The Racial Logic of Global Capitalism," in *Race, Empire, and the Crisis of the Subprime*, ed. Paula Chakravarty and Denise Ferreira da Silva, *American Quarterly* 64, no. 3 (September 2012): 361–385. https://doi.org/10.1353/aq.2012.0033; Stefano Harney and Fred Moten, *The Undercommons: Fugitive Planning and Black Study* (New York: Autonomedia, 2013); Hong, *The Ruptures in American Capital.*
29. Gus Lee, *China Boy* (New York: Plume, 1994.)
30. Amy Tan, *The Kitchen God's Wife* (New York: Putnam, 1991).
31. Carlos Bulosan, *America Is in the Heart* (Seattle: University of Washington Press, 2014).
32. John Phelan, *The Hispanization of the Philippines: Spanish Aims and Filipino Responses, 1565–1700* (Madison: University of Wisconsin Press, 2010).
33. Julia Alvarez, *How the Garcia Girls Lost Their Accents* (Chapel Hill: Algonquin Books, 1991); Esmeralda Santiago, *Cuando Era Puertorriqueña* (New York: Vintage Books, 1994); Anzaldúa, *Borderlands.*
34. The reader will notice that the adjectival "racialized gendered" is used quite frequently throughout the course of the argument. I rely on Lowe's feminist formulation of racialized capital and on Asian American cultural forms' coeval/immanent critique of global capitalism, both of which are central to my use of Filipino American studies, queer of color critique, Chicana feminist critique, and postcolonial disability as a coherent theoretical framework. Indeed, my readings of queerness, gender, and sexuality in Filipino-Chicano fictions demonstrate how Asian American materialist feminism and Chicana border theory are foundational optics underwriting, if overshadowed by, what we call queer of color critique.
35. Rhacel Parreñas, *Servants of Globalization: Migration and Domestic Work* (Stanford: Stanford University Press, 2015).

36. Spivak, *A Critique of Postcolonial Reason*, 283.
37. Spivak, *A Critique of Postcolonial Reason*, 275.
38. Put another way, "desire" allows us to get at different kinds of subjectivities, while "institutional historicism" flattens out subjectivity, difference, and bodily and linguistic specificity. Indeed, desire becomes the engine that animates the ills of ideological deception. Something like "false consciousness" is not due to being deceived but, rather, results from an undifferentiated desire; human subjectivity and consciousness as they interact with power transform into something like hegemony: one desires to be subjugated by the state or whatever. Spivak, a humanist highly skeptical of deterministic history à la Foucault, finds this problematic, not because false consciousness and hegemonic modes of compliance do not exist, but rather because this model of conceiving the subject is uncomplicated and does not take into account textured human differences.
39. Spivak, *A Critique of Postcolonial Reason*, 280.
40. Mendoza, *Metroimperial Intimacies*.
41. Spivak, *A Critique of Postcolonial Reason*, 280–281.
42. Brian Ascalon Roley, *American Son: A Novel* (New York: W. W. Norton & Company, 2001), 15.
43. Roley, *American Son*, 43.
44. Roley, *American Son*, 46.
45. Roley, *American Son*, 18.
46. The Asian American bottom has been approached from many angles. See David Eng, *Racial Castration Managing Masculinity in Asian America* (Durham: Duke University Press, 2001); Nguyen Tan Hoang, *A View from the Bottom: Asian American Masculinity and Sexual Representation* (Durham: Duke University Press, 2014); Joon Oluchi Lee, "The Joy of the Castrated Boy," *Social Text* 23, nos. 3–4 (2005): 35–56; Eng-Beng Lim, *Brown Boys and Rice Queens: Spellbinding Performance in the Asias* (New York: New York University Press, 2013); Mendoza, *Metroimperial Intimacies*.
47. Eng, *Racial Castration*, 1.
48. Victor Román Mendoza, *Metroimperial Intimacies: Fantasy, Racial-Sexual Governance, and the Philippines in U.S. Imperialism, 1899–1913* (Durham: Duke University Press, 2015); Eng-Beng Lim, *Brown Boys and Rice Queens: Spellbinding Performance in the Asias* (New York: New York University Press, 2014).
49. Roley, *American Son*, 87.
50. Roley, *American Son*, 86.
51. Roley, *American Son*, 87.
52. Roley, *American Son*, 50.
53. Roley, *American Son*, 54.
54. Anzaldúa, *Borderlands*, 83, 78.
55. Anzaldúa, *Borderlands*, 79.

56. Anzaldúa, *Borderlands*, 79.
57. Hsuan L. Hsu, *Sitting in the Darkness: Mark Twain's Asia and Comparative Racialization* (New York: New York University Press, 2015), 2.
58. For instance, many varieties of Chavacano Spanish are extinct and the others are basically endangered.
59. Kafer, *Feminist Queer Crip*.
60. Phelan, *The Hispanization of the Philippines*.
61. Anzaldúa, *Borderlands*.
62. Lauren Berlant, *Cruel Optimism* (Durham: Duke University Press, 2011).
63. Mitchell and Snyder, *Narrative Prosthesis*, 8.
64. Roley, *American Son*, 202.
65. Roley, *American Son*, 133–134.
66. Roley, *American Son*, 134.
67. Roley, *American Son*, 116.
68. Roley, *American Son*, 128.

## Chapter 3: Filipino Jose, Not Mexican José

1. Jose Antonio Vargas, *Dear America: Notes of an Undocumented Citizen* (New York: Dey Street Books, 2018), 141.
2. "Don't Call Jose Antonio Vargas an 'Immigration Activist,'" *Advocate*, December 16, 2015. http://www.advocate.com/40-under-40/2015/12/16/dont-call-jose-antonio-vargas-immigration-activist.
3. Vargas, *Dear America*, 165–166, 168, 173.
4. Vargas, *Dear America*, 166.
5. Vargas, *Dear America*, 71.
6. Dan Kosten, "Immigrants as Economic Contributors: Immigrant Tax Contributions and Spending Power," *National Immigration Forum*, September 6, 2018. https://immigrationforum.org/article/immigrants-as-economic-contributors-immigrant-tax-contributions-and-spending-power.
7. World Bank Group, "GDP (Current US$)—Philippines." https://data.worldbank.org/indicator/NY.GDP.MKTP.CD?locations=PH.
8. Kosten, "Immigrants as Economic Contributors."
9. Bill Chappell, "'A Day Without Immigrants' Promises a National Strike Thursday," *National Public Radio*, February 16, 2017. https://www.npr.org/sections/thetwo-way/2017/02/16/515555428/a-day-without-immigrants-promises-a-national-strike-thursday.
10. See Minich, *Accessible Citizenships*.
11. Vargas, *Dear America*, 168.
12. See Sarita See, *The Decolonized Eye: Filipino American Art and Performance* (Minneapolis: University of Minnesota Press, 2009); Dylan Rodríguez, *Suspended Apocalypse: White Supremacy, Genocide, and the Filipino Condition*

(Minneapolis: University of Minnesota Press, 2009); Isaac, *American Tropics*; Nerissa Balce, *Bodyparts of Empire: Visual Abjection, Filipino Images, and the American Archive* (Ann Arbor: University of Michigan Press, 2016).

13. Several works have discussed Filipinx and Latinx intersections. I particularly like: Guevarra, *Becoming Mexipino*; Ocampo, *Latinos of Asia*; Faye Caronan, *Legitimizing Empire: Filipino American and U.S. Puerto Rican Cultural Critique* (Urbana: University of Illinois Press, 2015).
14. Vargas, *Dear America*, 267.
15. Vargas, *Dear America*, 268.
16. Martin Joseph Ponce's notion of Philippine identity and cultural production being constitutively defined, due to the Philippines' multi-sited and multiracial history, through multiple modes of address greatly shaped the argument that I make here. While I do not focus on Anglophone literature from the Philippine archipelago, his critique of Filipinx American studies' unwillingness to engage with this archive has a notable resonance with the notion that Filipinx, Hispanic, and Latinx connections are not typically foregrounded. See Ponce, *Beyond the Nation*.
17. Vargas, *Dear America*, 223.
18. For significant baseline reading and innovative takes on the Asian American "model minority," see Rosalind S. Chou and Joe R. Feagin, *Myth of the Model Minority: Asian Americans Facing Racism*, 2nd ed. (New York: Routledge, 2016); Victor Bascara, *Model-Minority Imperialism* (Minneapolis: University of Minnesota Press, 2006); James Kyung-Jin Lee, *Pedagogies of Woundedness: Illness, Memoir, and the Ends of the Model Minority*, Dis/Color (Philadelphia: Temple University Press, 2022).
19. Vargas, *Dear America*, 268.
20. Lowe, *Immigrant Acts*; Ngai, *Impossible Subjects*.
21. Vargas, *Dear America*, 126.
22. Minich frames this as inaccessible citizenship in *Accessible Citizenships*. These arguments take some inspiration from Mitchell and Snyder, *Narrative Prosthesis*.
23. There is much work on this topic in US cultural studies of imperialism. Classic work includes Amy Kaplan, *The Anarchy of Empire in the Making of U.S. Culture* (Cambridge: Harvard University Press, 2002); Amy Kaplan and Donald E. Pease, *Cultures of United States Imperialism* (Durham: Duke University Press, 1993); Vicente L. Rafael, *White Love and Other Events in Filipino History* (Durham: Duke University Press, 2000).
24. Vargas, *Dear America*, 213–214.
25. Vargas, *Dear America*, 23.
26. This point resonates with work on "racialized gender," as theorized by Snorton in *Black on Both Sides*. I also cite here the queer potential of the x in Latinx. For me, as I elaborated in the introduction, this aligns with the antisocial thesis of queer theory, which promotes a negative disidentification with normative identity structures. Snorton—I think in conversation with Cathy Cohen—marks

this as a way of mapping affinity, not through stable identity claims, but through a common shared location of dispossession vis-à-vis the state. In this way, Latinx and Filipinx not only are queer in the sense of problematizing our investments in binary gender in Spanish morphologically, but also are racially queer in their co-formed disloyalty to stable ethno-racial identity.

27. Vargas, *Dear America*, 21.
28. Vargas, *Dear America*, 20.
29. Robyn Magalit Rodriguez, *Migrants for Export: How the Philippine State Brokers Labor to the World* (Minneapolis: University of Minnesota Press, 2010); Antonio T. Tiongson, Edgardo V. Gutierrez, and Ricardo V. Gutierrez, *Positively No Filipinos Allowed: Building Communities and Discourse* (Philadelphia: Temple University Press, 2006); Rick Baldoz, *The Third Asiatic: Empire and Migration in Filipino America, 1898–1946* (New York: New York University Press, 2011); Catherine Ceniza Choy, *Empire of Care: Nursing and Migration in Filipino American History* (Durham: Duke University Press, 2003).
30. Vargas, *Dear America*, 31–32.
31. See Anzaldúa, *Borderlands*; Saldaña-Portillo, *Indian Given*.
32. I interface with the idea of the "migrant imaginary" as theorized in Alicia R. Schmidt Camacho, *Migrant Imaginaries: Latino Cultural Politics in the U.S.-Mexico Borderlands*, Nation of Newcomers (New York: New York University Press). I am also thinking with Lisa Marie Cacho's *Social Death: Racialized Rightlessness and the Criminalization of the Unprotected* (New York: New York University Press, 2012). Cacho warns against the seductive thrall of respectability politics in rendering criminalized subjects unworthy of grief, mourning, or restitution. The linking of Mexicanness with criminality, while admittedly implicit in Vargas's progressive immigrant-affirmative narrative, is still very much at play when the endgame is US citizenship.
33. Tavia Amolo Ochieng' Nyongó and Joshua Takano Chambers-Letson, "Forward," in *The Sense of Brown*, by José Esteban Muñoz, Perverse Modernities (Durham: Duke University Press, 2020), xi.
34. Nyongó and Chambers-Letson, "Forward," in *The Sense of Brown*, xi.
35. Again, the notion of "social death" is derived from Cacho, *Social Death*.
36. See Robert L. Caserio, Lee Edelman, Judith Halberstam, José Esteban Muñoz, and Tim Dean, "The Antisocial Thesis in Queer Theory," *PMLA* 21, no. 3 (May 2006): 819–828.
37. Muñoz, *The Sense of Brown*, 3.
38. Muñoz, *The Sense of Brown*, 3, 63.
39. Judith Butler, "Imitation and Gender Insubordination," in *Deconstruction: Critical Concepts in Literary and Cultural Studies, Volume II*, ed. Jonathan Culler (New York: Routledge, 2003), 371–387. I should note that Butler was writing more specifically about feminism and the movement's shared definition of "woman."

40. See Eithne Luibhéid and Lionel Cantú, *Queer Migrations: Sexuality, U.S. Citizenship, and Border Crossings* (Minneapolis: University of Minnesota Press, 2005).
41. Vargas, *Dear America*, 40.
42. Vargas, *Dear America*, 122.
43. Sianne Ngai, *Ugly Feelings* (Cambridge: Harvard University Press, 2005).
44. I borrow the brilliant notion pondering the productive qualities of "maladjustment" from Cameron Awkward-Rich's monograph *The Terrible We: Thinking with Trans Maladjustment* (Durham: Duke University Press, 2022).
45. Ngai, *Ugly Feelings*, 11.
46. Vargas, *Dear America*, 95–96.
47. Nayan Shah, *Stranger Intimacies: Contesting Race, Sexuality, and the Law in the North American West* (Berkeley: University of California Press, 2011), 273.
48. Vargas, *Dear America*, 101.
49. Vargas, *Dear America*, 102.
50. Anderson, *Imagined Communities*.
51. Vargas, *Dear America*, 101–102.
52. Vargas, *Dear America*, 184.
53. Vargas, *Dear America*, 74.
54. Vargas, *Dear America*, 53.
55. Vargas, *Dear America*, 76–77. Emphasis added.
56. Vargas, *Dear America*, 75.
57. Therí Alyce Pickens, *Black Madness :: Mad Blackness* (Durham: Duke University Press, 2019).
58. Vargas, *Dear America*, 109.
59. Anne Cvetkovich, *Depression: A Public Feeling* (Durham: Duke University Press, 2012), 3.
60. For a brilliant engagement with the notion of "ethnographic entrapment," see Ferreira da Silva, *Towards a Global Idea of Race*.
61. La Marr Jurelle Bruce, *How to Go Mad Without Losing Your Mind: Madness and Black Radical Creativity*, Black Outdoors (Durham: Duke University Press, 2021).
62. Bruce, *How to Go Mad*, 2–3.
63. Saidiya Hartman, *Lose Your Mother: A Journey Along the Atlantic Slave Route* (New York: Farrar, Straus & Giroux, 2008).
64. Vargas, *Dear America*, 223.
65. Vargas, *Dear America*, 224.
66. Vargas, *Dear America*, 195.
67. Vargas, *Dear America*, 199–200.
68. "Examined Life—Judith Butler & Sunaura Taylor," October 6, 2010. https://www.youtube.com/watch?v=koHZaPkF6qE.
69. Vargas, *Dear America*, 96.

70. Vargas, *Dear America*, 204–205.
71. Vargas, *Dear America*, 206.
72. Vargas, *Dear America*, 206.
73. Vargas, *Dear America*, 205.
74. M. Jacqui Alexander, *Pedagogies of Crossing: Meditations on Feminism, Sexual Politics, Memory, and the Sacred*, Perverse Modernities (Durham: Duke University Press), 6.
75. Vargas, *Dear America*, 207.
76. Jason De León, *The Land of Open Graves: Living and Dying on the Migrant Trail* (Berkeley: University of California Press, 2015).
77. Vargas, *Dear America*, 208.
78. Vargas, *Dear America*, 214.
79. Anderson, *Imagined Communities*.
80. For more on this, see Ferguson, *The Reorder of Things*.
81. Reddy, *Freedom with Violence*.

## Chapter 4: Mad Migrant Imaginary

1. Hisko Hulsing, *Undone*, Amazon Prime Original, 2019. https://www.amazon.com/Undone-Season-1/dp/B0875GVR67. When this chapter was written a second season of the show aired. The content of this chapter will focus only on the first season given the complexity of its themes and richness of the narrative.
2. Schmidt Camacho, *Migrant Imaginaries*.
3. *Diagnostic and Statistical Manual of Mental Disorders*, 5th ed. (Arlington: American Psychiatric Association, 2013), 87.
4. Glen O. Gabbard, *Psychodynamic Psychiatry in Clinical Practice*, 2nd edition (Washington, DC: American Psychiatric Press, 1994), 173–174.
5. Gabbard, *Psychodynamic Psychiatry*, 174.
6. Gabbard, *Psychodynamic Psychiatry*, 174.
7. This field is becoming more and more expansive. See Kim, *Curative Violence*; Alison Kafer and Eunjung Kim, "Disability and the Edges of Intersectionality." In *99682*, ed. Clare Barker and Stuart Murray, Cambridge Companions to Literature (Cambridge: Cambridge University Press, 2018), 123–138; Sami Schalk and Jina B. Kim, "Integrating Race, Transforming Feminist Disability Studies." *SIGNS* 46, no. 1 (2020): 31–55. https://doi.org/10.1086/709213.
8. Burch, *Committed*.
9. Anzaldúa, *Borderlands*.
10. Susan Burch and Alison Kafer, *Deaf and Disability Studies: Interdisciplinary Perspectives* (Washington, DC: Gallaudet University Press, 2010).
11. Many Deaf individuals would opt for "Deaf" with a capital "D," which is meant to highlight ties to the ethnolinguistic identity of Deaf culture. It is helpful to

think of this like a national demonym, e.g. "Japanese," "Estonian," "Deaf." This distinguishes Deaf culture and language from the pathologized medical condition of "deaf" originating from the chauvinism of hearing culture. In this chapter, I will opt to use "Deaf" when referring to this community but will maintain the use of "deaf" when referring to the physical difference of being hard-of-hearing.

12. Karen Nakamura, *Deaf in Japan: Signing and the Politics of Identity* (Ithaca: Cornell University Press, 2006); Douglas C. Baynton, *Forbidden Signs: American Culture and the Campaign against Sign Language* (Chicago: University of Chicago Press, 1996).
13. "Normate" is a term that specifically refers to able-bodied normativity. It was coined by Rosemarie Garland-Thomson. See Garland-Thomson, *Extraordinary Bodies*.
14. Gabbard, *Psychodynamic Psychiatry*.
15. Anzaldúa, *Borderlands*.
16. Kareem Khubchandani, *Ishtyle: Accenting Gay Indian Nightlife*, Triangulations (Ann Arbor: University of Michigan Press, 2020).
17. Muñoz, *The Sense of Brown*.
18. Shah, *Stranger Intimacy*.
19. Shah, *Stranger Intimacy*, 55.
20. Schalk and Kim, "Integrating Race."
21. Shah, *Stranger Intimacy*, 273.
22. Jeffrey J. Martin, "Supercrip Identity," in *Handbook of Disability Sport and Exercise Psychology* (New York: Oxford University Press, 2017), 139–148. https://doi.org/10.1093/oso/9780190638054.003.0015.
23. Martin, "Supercrip Identity."
24. Lowe, *Immigrant Acts*; Grace Kyungwon Hong, *The Ruptures of American Capital: Women of Color Feminism and the Culture of Immigrant Labor* (Minneapolis: University of Minnesota Press, 2006); Ngai, *Impossible Subjects*.
25. María Josefina Saldaña-Portillo, *The Revolutionary Imagination in the Americas and the Age of Development*, Latin America Otherwise (Durham: Duke University Press, 2003), 286.
26. Alexandra Stern, *Eugenic Nation: Faults and Frontiers of Better Breeding in Modern America*, American Crossroads 17 (Oakland: University of California Press, 2016).
27. José Vasconcelos, *La Raza Cósmica: Misión de La Raza Iberoamericana, Argentina y Brasil*, Colección Austral (Mexico City: Espasa-Calpe Mexicana, 1948), 802.
28. Audra Simpson, *Mohawk Interruptus: Political Life Across the Borders of Settler States* (Durham: Duke University Press, 2014); J. Kēhaulani Kauanui, " 'A Structure, Not an Event': Settler Colonialism and Enduring Indigeneity," *Lateral* 5, no. 1 (Spring 2016). http://csalateral.org/issue/5-1/forum-alt-humanities-settler-colonialism-enduring-indigeneity-kauanui.

29. On such predispositions in Western society, see Michel Foucault, *Madness and Civilization: A History of Insanity in the Age of Reason* (New York: Pantheon Books, 1965).
30. Anzaldúa, *Borderlands*.
31. Burch, *Committed*, 10.
32. Geoffrey Reaume, "From the Perspectives of Mad People," in *The Routledge History of Madness and Mental Health*, ed. Greg Eghigian, Routledge Histories (New York: Routledge, 2017), 277–296; Anna Mollow, "'When Black Women Start Going on Prozac': Race, Gender, and Mental Illness in Meri Nana-Ama Danquah's *Willow Weep for Me*," *MELUS* 31, no. 3 (September 2006): 67; Bruce, *How to Go Mad*; Pickens, *Black Madness*.
33. Burch, *Committed*.
34. Juliana Hu Pegues, *Space-Time Colonialism: Alaska's Indigenous and Asian Entanglements*, Critical Indigeneities (Chapel Hill: University of North Carolina Press, 2021).
35. Hu Pegues, *Space-Time Colonialism*, 13.
36. Day, *Alien Capital*; Jodi A. Byrd, *The Transit of Empire: Indigenous Critiques of Colonialism*, First Peoples: New Directions Indigenous (Minneapolis: University of Minnesota Press, 2011); Lowe, *The Intimacies of Four Continents*.

# Index

Page numbers in *italics* refer to figures.